Performing for Motion Capture

Performing for Motion Capture

A Guide for Practitioners

John Dower and Pascal Langdale

methuen | drama

LONDON • NEW YORK • OXFORD • NEW DELHI • SYDNEY

METHUEN DRAMA
Bloomsbury Publishing Plc
50 Bedford Square, London, WC1B 3DP, UK
1385 Broadway, New York, NY 10018, USA
29 Earlsfort Terrace, Dublin 2, Ireland

BLOOMSBURY, METHUEN DRAMA and the Methuen Drama logo are
trademarks of Bloomsbury Publishing Plc

First published in Great Britain 2022

Cover design: Ben Anslow
Photos by Archis Achrekar. Courtesy of Centroid Motion Capture &
Faceware Technologies

A catalogue record for this book is available from the British Library.

A catalog record for this book is available from the Library of Congress

ISBN: HB: 978-1-3502-1126-1
      PB: 978-1-3502-1125-4
      ePDF: 978-1-3502-1127-8
      eBook: 978-1-3502-1128-5

Typeset by RefineCatch Limited, Bungay, Suffolk

To find out more about our authors and books visit www.bloomsbury.com
and sign up for our newsletters.

Contents

1 What is motion capture? 1
We define the technology and the challenges ahead in this
exciting and significant performance medium.
John Dower and Pascal Langdale

2 The body 25
How to develop a responsive, free and versatile instrument.
Pascal Langdale

3 Imaginary environments 53
We explore the limits of our imagination and
professionalizing play.
Pascal Langdale

4 Mocap is an animated medium 67
The pure, simple and ruthlessly honest information that is at the
heart of the process: How the actor is one part of a team of
artists behind the animated character and how your
performance is manipulated after capture.
John Dower

Figures

Contributors

Kim Baumann Larsen is CEO and founder of Dimension Design, a virtual architecture and VR production studio in Norway. Educated as an architect, he started his career in VR in Houston 25 years ago. For the past ten years, he has designed, produced and published narrative real-time, AR and VR experiences. In his virtual architecture he blends the science of environmental psychology with the art of visual storytelling to create comfortable and inspiring spaces for work and play. Kim is a curator for the architecture track of the RealTime Conference and co-founder of XR Norway and Norwegian Interactive Storytellers.

Kezia Burrows is an actor. She studied at RADA and works in theatre, television, film and voice over; and in video games since 2009, whether as the whole character: voice, likeness and performance capture, to motion capture only, to solely voice. Her work covers the whole spectrum from independent games to AAA. Working on over 100 games, she loves this medium and has been in the fortunate position to watch it evolve both creatively and technically over the years.

Alex Coulombe, an architect turned XR-chitect, is a designer, developer and educator who has worked in VR/AR/Realtime for over 10 years. After developing the world's first virtual reality system for evaluating theatre sightlines at Fisher Dachs Associates, he co-founded the NYC-based creative studio, Agile Lens. A rising XR thought leader, Alex and his company's work features at conferences around the world. He has taught at Syracuse University, NYU Tisch, and as an authorized Unreal Engine instructor for Epic Games. He is an organizer of the 5th Wall Forum and the RealTime Conference. Follow him on Twitter and YouTube @iBrews.

Stéphane Dalbera (founder and owner of Atopos) trained as a scientist, and has been a pioneer in the use of motion capture and real-time 3D for video games, cinema, science and the performing arts for over 20 years with his company Atopos.

'If you've played a video game, you've probably killed me.'
Richard Dorton, aka Mocapman, is a veteran performance capture actor, director, stunt coordinator, producer, movement consultant instructor and casting director with over 100 video game credits to his name. Richard has brought to life iconic video game characters like Darth Vader, Master Chief, Nathan Drake, Peter Venkman and creatures from games like *Left 4 Dead 1* and *2*, *Silent Hill: Homecoming*, *Ghostbusters* and many more. Feature films include *Jack the Giant Killer*, *Spiderman*, *Tron* and 'Kevin', the left head of King Ghidorah in *Godzilla: King of the Monsters*. Richard also runs the US division of The Mocap Vaults.

David Footman joined the film industry in Vancouver in the early nineties, galvanizing his love of storytelling. He joined the DGA at 30 years old and started working on high-profile visual effects pictures like *X-Men* and *iRobot*. After supervising the motion capture on *iRobot* and helping close the FX shots in LA, David was introduced to the Electronic Arts team in San Francisco making *The Lord of the*

Rings: The Third Age (RPG). Directing 250 scenes from the Tolkien world is still the highlight of his career, and marked the beginning of his journey in games. In this exciting technical landscape David searches for story and performance in worlds that inspire play.

Oliver Hollis-Leick has had twenty years in the mocap business, and has performed in over a hundred titles that include *Call of Duty*, *Halo*, *Quantum Break* and *Destiny*, playing characters like Iron Man, Master Chief, Agent 47, James Bond and the Hulk. Oliver studied acting at the Bristol Old Vic Theatre School but in 2012 he began to work in narrative design and writing for video games and has since become the creative director at Saber Interactive. He is also co-founder of The Mocap Vaults, and has taught mocap acting in the UK, US and Europe.

Hideaki Itsuno (game director, Capcom) joined Capcom in 1994, and his works as a video game director include *Devil May Cry* series, *Capcom vs. SNK* series, *Street Fighter Alpha*, *Dragon's Dogma*, among others.

Jessica Jefferies is a casting director who works primarily within VFX and SFX. Her speciality is pinpointing specific skill sets and physical attributes which lend themselves to the world of performance capture, prosthetics and creature performance.

With over 8 years experience as one of Europe's leading performance capture actors, Jessica now works directly with studios, developers and production houses to find the best talent for this incredible, expanding part of the arts.

Jessica's recent credits include *Peaky Blinders* (VR), *Unknown9: Awakening* (video game), *Little Hope* (video game) and *Warhammer 40K* (VR).

Steve Kniebihly is a veteran cinematic director with a passion for directing actors, camera work and editing. Over the span of an 18yrs+ career Steve has directed projects in Europe, the US, Canada and Japan and used performance capture and his deep knowledge of narrative techniques to help craft amazing stories and bring to life memorable characters in some critically acclaimed AAA games. His work includes: *Heavy Rain, Beyond: Two Souls, The Witcher 3: Blood and Wine, Planet of the Apes: Last Frontier, Resident Evil 3* (remake) and *Resident Evil Village*, amongst others.

Ben Lumsden is the business development manager for media and entertainment at Epic Games, where he has furthered Unreal Engine adoption and innovation in EMEA since 2017. Ben has worked on films *District 9* and *Rise of the Planet of the Apes*, and games *Tom Clancy's Splinter Cell: Blacklist* and *Dead Rising 3*. He's earned credits on *Star Wars: The Force Awakens, Avengers: Age of Ultron, Godzilla*, and the game *Star Citizen*. Ben was also instrumental in launching the Royal Shakespeare Company's *The Tempest* in which the character Ariel puppeteered a live avatar on stage, rendered in real time in Unreal Engine.

Paul-William Mawhinney was born and raised in Australia where he graduated from the National Institute of Dramatic Art (Sydney) with a Bachelor of Dramatic Art. His career spans work in theatre, film, television, voice-overs and performance capture for numerous AAA video game titles and animation. More recently, he has begun to turn his hand to writing and directing. Paul-William teaches acting for performance capture at some of the most prestigious and well-established arts training institutions around the world, including; Drama Studio London (UK), Bristol Old Vic Theatre School (UK), Filmakademie (Germany) and the Western Australian Academy of Performing Arts.

Jeremy Meunier (motion capture lead at MOOV, Squeeze Animation) sped up his career in 2005 with the massive motion-captured video-game *Heavy Rain*. With both solid theoretical and technical background (anatomy, perception of movement, rigging, scripting), he's been consulted to design and develop robust mocap pipelines, leading the motion capture department of several studios (Quantic Dream, Dontnod, Guerilla Games) and mocap services providers (Atopos, Solidanim, Game On, Squeeze).

He's been credited for some famous video games (*Heavenly Sword, Life Is Strange S1, Vampyr, Outlast II, Dishonored*) and feature films (*Deadpool 2, Murder On the Orient Express, 10'000 BC, Race*). He has been an occasional lecturer for some 3D schools and universities in France.

Goran Milic's first full time job in the industry was in 2004 as a mocap tracker at Centroid Motion Capture. Next step was Weta Digital where he spent an amazing 11.5 years working on some of the legendary VFX films like *Avatar, The Hobbit* trilogy, the *Planet of the Apes* films, *The BFG, Alita – Battle Angel* and others. Specializing in facial mocap working on set, and facial animation back at the office, he became head of the facial motion department. Since 2018, Goran has worked at Goodbye Kansas studios in Sweden as head of facial animation.

Gilles Monteil, if everything had been as planned, would still be on the stage today, writing his plays for his small theatre company 'Le Tribunal de Poche', continuing his quest for the realistic physical actor. In 1997 he saw a mocap acting job advertised at Ubisoft, but ended up being hired as a 3D animator. He started at the Montreal animation studio as a director and later animation director on *Splinter Cell, Far Cry, The Division*, and *Watch Dog* franchises. In 2005 he created UBI Montreal's Vicon mocap studio, and sometimes can be found in the volume continuing his quest for the realistic physical actor.

Marc Morisseau is an experienced performance capture specialist whose skills range from data processing to stage management. His game titles include *Resident Evil 6*, *Call of Duty: Modern Warfare* and *Titanfall*, while his films include *The Mazerunner*, Marvel's *Ant-Man* and James Cameron's *Avatar* sequels. Since breaking into the industry in 2011, he's constantly seeking the forefront of performance capture technologies to help propel the industry forward in innovative solutions for creativity in a technical space.

Ralph Palmer has spent much of his career working in what they now call 'Old School 2D', from TV specials to TV series and on to feature films (currently numbering 22 full features) such as *An American Tail*, *'Land Before Time*, *All Dogs Go To Heaven*, *Pocahontas*, *The Hunchback of Notre Dame* and *Atlantis*, then learning 3D leading to *Mickey's Philharmagic*, *Garfield*, and even *Scooby Doo*.

He successfully moved into video games as animation director with the *Harry Potter* franchise. After the groundbreaking *Quantum Break* with Remedy/Microsoft, he taught advanced visual arts at Breda University of Applied Science. He is currently head of animation at Rebellion.

Kate Saxon directs video games, as well as theatre, television and film. She was awarded a place in the inaugural *BAFTA Elevate*, with her work recognized particularly for excellence in directing performances for games. Kate has directed performance capture shoots and voice for innumerable games, including twice BAFTA nominated *Mafia III*; 2016 BAFTA winner *Everybody's Gone To The Rapture*; 2015 BAFTA winner *Alien: Isolation; Witcher 2* and *Witcher 3* (most nominated game: Game Awards 2015); *Fable 2*, *Fable 3*; *Little Big Planet 3*; and *Hitman*. Kate was also the director for the UK casting and trailers of *Cyberpunk*.

Jeasy Sehgal is the founder of Graphic Monk Ltd, a multi-disciplinary production house with multiple brands incorporated under the umbrella, Imperial Swords, The Imperial School of Swordsmanship, Dynakinetix: Motion Capture and Virtual Productions. He is based in Dunedin, New Zealand. www.GraphicMonk.com

Yuji Shimomura graduated from *Kurata Action Club,* and then worked beside Donnie Yen in Hong Kong as a stuntman. He has worked as an action director and film director as well as working on *U'den Frameworks* and his work as an action director can be seen in various fields such as movies, commercials and video games.

Video games: *Devil May Cry 3, Devil May Cry 4, Bayonetta, Metal Gear Solid V: The Phantom Pain,* and *Devil May Cry 5.*

Films: *Death Trance, Gantz: Perfect Answer, Library War, I AM A HERO, Re:Born, Bleach, Kingdom, Crazy Samurai: 400 vs. 1,* which features 77-minute, one-scene, no-cut action sequence, and *Alice in Borderland* for Netflix.

Bryan Steagall was born in Seguin, Texas on 5 August 1969, moved to Mexico City at 3 weeks old and stayed there until age 18, when his family moved back to the United States. Studied for a Bachelor of Arts in Metals (Art Jewelry) at the University of Texas El Paso.

Brian began his journey with motion capture in 2007 as an alpha/beta tester for Optitrack and from there fell in love with the technology and is now a distributor for Dynamixyz, Optitrack, Stretchsense and Rokoko. He has been married to his wife Eva for 28 years and they have 2 adult sons.

Gareth Taylor is an innovative and experienced director, movement director, performer and teacher. After training as an actor at Guildford

School of Acting he travelled to the prestigious École Internationale de Théâtre Jacques Lecoq, Paris. For 20 years he has been working in film and video games as a performer with over 30 AAA credits including EA, Warner Bros, Sony, Supermassive and Disney. He is also working as a performance director, AD and movement specialist. Gareth is a creative associate for the multi award-winning theatre company Curious Directive and a movement associate for The Mocap Vaults.

Mari Ueda and **Kumiko Ogawa** founded Pivot Motion Inc., located in Los Angeles, California, as a production company that provides professional services for clients' motion capture, performance capture, voice-recording, casting and other production needs. With the experience of running a Hollywood motion capture/voice-over studio, Both Kumiko Ogawa and Mari Ueda are Japanese–English bilingual producers.

With a combined 20 years of experience working as producers with top tier clients, actors and vendors in the motion capture industry, they are experienced in providing professional, unique and flexible production services that fit each client's needs.

America Young has worked on over 65 video games titles from *Spider-Man* to *Halo 5*, *Saints Row* to *Sunset Overdrive* and *Call of Duty*. She is currently working as Batgirl in the new *Gotham Knights* video from WB Games. Most recently, she directed the vertical slice of the hit game *Resident Evil Village* that broke all sale records for Capcom. She also directed the critically acclaimed season of the Barbie motion capture animated series, *Barbie Vlog*, for Mattel which was featured on *VICE*, *Vogue*, *Glamour* and *Newsweek* among others. It has been viewed on YouTube over 110 million times and inspired kids of all ages across the world.

Actor Credits (Images)

Ace Ruele is a professional actor who is known in the VFX/motion capture industry for his movement/creature acting abilities. His creature work has been featured in a number films and video games, working with companies, such as Marvel, WarnerBros, Amazon, Supermassive Games and Deep Sliver. In 2020 he founded Creature Bionics, which develops performance rigs for actors to be able to match the skeleton of a specific creature, which enhances their performance, and creates better reference and motion capture data.

Alexandra Guelff is an actor who trained at RADA. She works across a broad range of theatre (*Witness for the Prosecution*), film (*Brimstone*), TV (*Call the Midwife*) and games (*Game of Thrones*).

Acknowledgements

Thanks to all of our interviewees, in particular our fellow mocap teachers – Paul-William Mawhinney, Gareth Taylor and Marc Morisseau. We could not have written this book without you.

Thanks to our agent Michael Levine for faith and good humour.

Thanks to Mari Ueda and Kumiko Ogawa for translation, and Gilles Monteil for accepting our every call with generosity and patience.

Thanks to Anna Brewer and Sam Nicholls at Bloomsbury for support and encouragement.

Thanks to Archis Achrekar for great photos, Eden Bø Dower for graphics, Alex Guelff and Ace Ruele for time and talent, and Iain Sylvester, Phil Stilgoe and the team at Centroid Motion Capture for hosting us.

Special mentions need to go to Richard Dorton who has hugely advanced teaching in the United States and the trailblazer Oliver Hollis-Leick, who has led the development of mocap workshops from the start.

Finally, thanks to Eli Bø who suggested we write this book and Erin Kell for tea and encouragement in a cold Toronto.

John Dower and Pascal Langdale
London and Toronto

1

What is motion capture?

JOHN DOWER AND PASCAL LANGDALE

To know what to do in the motion capture studio ('the volume') you need knowledge and understanding, just as you would if acting for the camera or the stage. Motion capture (mocap) is simply a new and unique acting medium and this book is going to give you the tools to create compelling and believable characters in the volume. We will explain what motion capture is, the similarities and differences between other performance media and how it fits into the digital production process. In doing so, we'll look at the history and development of the medium with a brief explanation on how it works. We'll then give a snapshot on how it is evolving and being used increasingly in video games, films, television, virtual reality and live events. We hope that you will start to appreciate that if you don't get an understanding of this medium, there is a danger you will be left behind.

Contributors – Stéphane Dalbera (mocap supervisor, mocap consultant), Jeremy Meunier (motion capture lead at MOOV, Squeeze Animation) and Gilles Monteil (realization director, animator, movement specialist, Ubisoft Montpellier).

What made you pick up this book? What has brought students flocking to acting for mocap classes worldwide? Is this a fad, an acting medium that will soon be proved an 'imposter' or one that deserves its own Oscar category?

There has been much hubris and dismissal of the art of performing for motion capture from industry figures around the world. Outrageous claims of what mocap can do and what it means are often met with eyebrow raises from doubters and equally arrogant shakes of the head from evangelists.

We position ourselves in the middle of these arguments. As open-minded practitioners we are less interested in the hype but more in what this new medium actually offers and how best to work with it.

We argue in this book there are some truths about motion capture performance that are regularly ignored, foremost of which is that it is an acting medium in its own right. An acting medium that exists inside digital virtual production, which is transforming the way humans tell stories.

What is different about working in motion capture as a performer? What exactly is digital and virtual production? Our book will set out to answer these questions and many more, giving you acting advice, exercises and technical understanding from both an actor's *and* a director's perspective.

Some chapters are written by a director, some by an actor, giving you a sense of how our individual experiences have shaped our approaches. We believe that this gives the book a unique strength given that mocap demands a much greater cross discipline collaboration, as different departments can have an equal say about what is desired, or even possible, in performance. No performer's character creation is untouched by other creators, making the director's perspective the vital bridge between animator and performer.

There are chapters that will speak more directly to actors and performers, some that will also speak to directors wishing to get into mocap, to animators wishing to improve their directing skills and to technicians hoping to get more of a sense of how to help create good performances. We think the book will appeal to creatives working in several different areas of mocap production.

However, we also hope to give an overview, an objective sense of the medium, by demystifying and explaining the basics, drawing on the experiences and expertise of established practitioners – actors, animators, directors, technicians and wizards working in motion capture. Read this book and we think you will agree that motion capture *is* the performance medium of its time.

Motion capture is a medium in its own right

So, what differentiates performing in motion capture from performing on the stage, or for the camera? For Andy Serkis acting for motion capture is 'pure acting' because it requires huge leaps of imagination and commitment to an imagined world. In motion capture, you can play anything – a human, an ape, a monster, even a tree! Your body can drive any conceivable character or 'rigged' object. Your looks, skin colour, age and even sometimes gender are irrelevant because your likeness is usually not being captured – your movement, your motion, is.

So, where do we start our training? Just as we would not expect a stage actor to start immediately working on a stage, or a film actor in front of a camera, we always start with our students in a rehearsal room so they can absorb what mocap requires of them – for it truly is an acting medium in its own right.

For mocap supervisor Stéphane Dalbera, the definition of the performance in mocap is 'to respect the dynamic of motion'. For Jeremy Meunier, mocap is 'a way to express feelings through body and facial language'. Purely technically, mocap is the capture of human-derived movement for analysis and use in digital production. So, how does it work? How does it record the performer's movement? What is preserved? What is discarded? By the end of this chapter, you will have a clear idea of what mocap is, how it works, why you need to consider taking it further and what this book will offer you.

So, hold on to your hats! We will be deconstructing and redefining what acting is. Actors often define themselves by the medium they tend to work in and though there is a certain amount of movement between stage and screen, many actors specialize in one area and define themselves as such. Moreover, we live in a social media dominated world that often defines performers, animators, directors and other creatives by their appearance, thus creating a known brand for their work. Actors get cast for body type, by gender, race, age, looks. However, mocap looks past almost all of that and allows the actor to inhabit completely different characters from themselves. Let's go back in the history of acting to see what we can take as inspiration for our approach to performing for mocap.

A long time ago, the body was accepted as a vessel to communicate with the Gods. The Greeks and Romans invented mime and played it for centuries in big arenas, where the talking was done by the 'choir'. However, as religions progressed in the West, the body began to be increasingly seen as taboo. An exception can be seen in a form such as pantomime, which appeared when actors who were performing

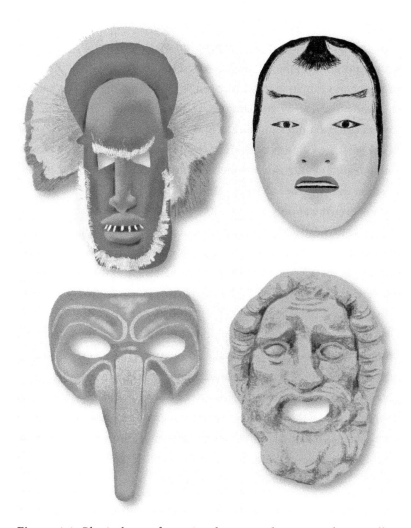

Figure 1.1 *Physical transformation has existed since we began telling stories. Masks have been used for centuries as a way of creating character in theatre. Complementary physicality is essential. (Dogon dance mask from Mali, Noh Theatre, Japan, Commedia Dell' Arte and Greek Theatre mask. Artwork by Eden Bø Dower.)*

caricatures were forbidden to speak on stage. When silent movies came about, physical bodily expression was briefly the paramount skill required until the talkies arrived in the 1930s and the voice took precedence. Only in animation, born at the same time as cinema, did the body survive as a main vessel of expression. In acting, the knowledge and understanding of body movement technique – at least in the West – was long constrained by religious belief in the weakness, immodesty and untrustworthiness of the flesh, and later its subservient position to the higher value of mind and psychology.

However, it was only ever possible to push it away into the margins. While Noh Theatre has been performed along the same physical rules for hundreds of years, Europe had the chaotic improvised physical archetypes of Commedia. That style persisted into, for example, Molière plays and then found an explosion of opportunity in silent movies.

As an example, Charlie Chaplin and Buster Keaton used to have a competition to see who could make a movie with the fewest expository and speech cards. This was because they prided themselves on being able to effectively tell a complete story through physicality and facial expression of all the characters on the screen.[1] The advent of sound in films changed all that, so acting became more inward, or what we might call 'inside-out'. Head of animation at Ubisoft and movement expert, Gilles Monteil points out that, then:

> The talkies prioritised text at the expense of action. When the silent era was replaced by the introduction of sound, the technological change completely changed acting technique. However, the tradition of movement was kept alive by animators. With the advent of motion capture, there is a new era of actors finding the importance of actions in acting. The tradition and knowledge exist, but there remains no acting school for motion capture actors.

Many actors do not have the tools, teaching or precedents to know how to perform in it.

Our challenge is to inspire and educate a new generation of digital performers, to be part of a movement which proves to actors that acting for mocap is *real acting* and takes great skill, ability and dedication to achieve.

Digital and virtual production

Motion capture technology has developed to what it is today largely as a result of the advances in digital production. Work began in the 1970s to compress and digitize video images, and by the late 1980s digital video formats were coming on stream. Digital media can be created, viewed, distributed, modified and preserved on digital electronic devices, which has revolutionized the television industry, and more recently the film industry.

Digital production requires digital 'assets' to manipulate – assets can be elements of environments, props or characters themselves. Character assets can be created on any visual format and be digitized onto digital formats to be animated or motion captured. They are then placed inside a digital virtual environment, where they can be further manipulated. Since the advent of digital video and the exponential rise of video games, digital visual effects ('VFX') and environments have greatly increased the tools at the disposal of both games designers and filmmakers.

Digital production allowed another phenomenon – the notion of non-linear production, where elements and structure could be changed instantaneously at almost any point. Film and TV editing became revolutionized by digital processes which replaced physical cutting in film and time-consuming duplication in video. Video games took this a stage further as computing power enabled increasingly complex gameplay and interactive narrative.

We have started to become used to seeing a cross fertilization between the *linear* storytelling tradition of film and television and that of the *interactive* storytelling medium best showcased in games. However, it has been games developers who have mostly been the most open minded about bringing in storytellers from the film and TV world while their more traditional counterparts have rested on their more established laurels. The snobbishness and ignorance we have encountered over the years from more traditional peers has been shameful. The film and TV industry has looked down on the games industry for too long as an inferior medium, merely seeing opportunities for making film versions of games. They have had to take notice as the games business far outstripped the film industry in terms of revenues. However, it has been in the advent of films utilizing game engines, also known as real-time engines, that they have really had to wake up and smell the coffee.

What is a game engine or real-time engine?

While you are playing a video game, a complex computer system is allowing you to go down that mountain stream or climb that building, or enter that cave at your very whim. The game engine is arranging the animation, the environment, the sound, the lighting to respond to the player's direction. The real-time engine enables your interaction and responds to your decisions from the game controller live – in 'real-time'. It takes a powerful and complex engine to respond in such an immediate way and currently the main companies involved in real-time engines are Unreal from Epic Games[2] and Unity.[3] These engines allow anyone to use them, are relatively easy to use and program, and importantly allow both beginners and the more experienced to use them right up to a professional level. *Star Wars Jedi: Fallen Order* and *Warhammer 40,000: Eternal Crusade* were made using the Unreal game engine, and *Fortnite* is its biggest credit.

Their advent has been revolutionary for the film and TV industry, because now a virtual world can be created relatively easily and decisions made as the project progresses. Gone are the days when an animated film had to be made as a storyboard first and then laboriously recreated stage by stage, meaning that as the project developed changes were difficult. Now, a virtual world can be created and scenes can be animated, shot using motion capture or live action and then manipulated all within the virtual environment. Think of a film such as Disney's recent *The Jungle Book*, which was made in Unity. Think of the recent *Star Wars* films which have their environments digitally created, so it becomes natural for the director to strap on a VR (virtual reality) headset and explore the sets in 3D. Then they decide on blocking and camera positions in a digital world, which can be changed and manipulated even after shooting the performances.

When we first started working in motion capture the notion that we could decide on camera positions and lenses *after* the shooting was mind blowing. For an experienced film director, being freed from being locked down to simultaneous performance and camera decisions is a liberation. For actors, it brings us back to a world of pure imagination, unencumbered by playing for a camera or audience. Digital virtual production in a real-time engine has facilitated this and finally film and television makers have woken up to a new reality. Live action shoots are regularly using set extensions and replacements and visual effects are facilitated by virtual production and real-time engines. Given that digital production has become a reality and that these techniques have raised production values while becoming cheaper all the time, there is no way we are going back to the way things were. This is where motion captured animation resides and is developing, being refined and becoming ever more sophisticated.

Motion capture – the technical lowdown in a nutshell

Motion capture as we know it today was first used over a hundred years ago in a process called rotoscoping, developed by animator Max Fleischer, in which filmed performances were traced over by animators to create more life-like animations. This was famously first used in a movie in Walt Disney's *Snow White and the Seven Dwarfs* in 1939.

By the late 1950s, animators were experimenting with potentiometers (adjustable resistors) to record an actor's movement for display on a television screen, and by the 1980s they were using bodysuits lined with active markers with cameras to track movement. This technique was also used by scientists and medical experts to analyse the gait of athletes and war veterans to further understand the effects of injuries on the body.

Even as late as the 1990s, motion capture technology was rudimentary and there was much more work to do for the animators than there is now in cleaning up the data in every frame. This painstaking process was streamlined and improved so that, by the turn of the century, motion capture was becoming increasingly sophisticated and often used by the medical community for movement analysis, while the appearance of Gollum in *The Lord of the Rings: The Fellowship of the Ring* in 2001, played by Andy Serkis was what really put motion capture as we know it on the map.

The important concept to get over here is that what all motion capture systems are looking to capture is – the skeleton. Human skin, muscles, body shape, clothes – none of this is captured. Purely and simply – just the skeleton! The digital skin of a character is then applied to the skeleton, which in turn then drives the character. So, the performer is acting as a puppeteer – their movement is driving their digital avatar.

This is the moment in introductory classes when students often gape. Some of them might secretly be thinking – so, if the system only captures my skeleton and it can't see me, my performance is anonymized, it's no longer me – so does my performance really show? This book is going to prove to you that it really does show and that it really does matter. But before we do, let's just be clear as to how the technology works because if you understand that, it will all begin to fit into place. What follows is a basic explanation. You may want to study this subject deeper, but we want to get the principles over.

There are three main modes of motion capture, all seeking to capture the skeleton:

1 Optical or line-of-sight capture

2 Inertial capture

3 Markerless capture

Optical or line-of-sight capture

This is likely to be the method you have seen most coverage of to advertise the films and games that utilize it. It's also identified by the figure-hugging Lycra® suits covered in reflective markers. Using infra-red cameras which surround the studio, the markers' positions in space are captured to a high degree of accuracy and then turned into a 3D cloud of dots that correlate with the skeleton and joints of the performer. This 'cloud data' moves through space as the performer moves and this is recorded.

Figure 1.2 *Optical mocap – actors wearing mocap suits with reflectors. (Photo by Archis Achrekar. Courtesy of Centroid Motion Capture.)*

The space in which the actor's movements can be captured is defined by a 3-dimensional area which the cameras can cover. It is called 'the volume' and is often split up into 1-metre squares in a grid pattern on the floor, so that performers, sets and props can be accurately placed in the space.

It's the most accurate and expensive way of capturing mocap data. It is also possible to shoot outdoors using 'active' LED markers rather than the 'passive' reflective ones used in the studio, enabling shooting in daylight and in real locations. You may have seen videos of Andy Serkis in the recent *Planet of the Apes* movies that use this technology.

Well-known manufacturers include – Vicon, Motion Analysis and OptiTrack.

Figure 1.3 *Centroid Motion Capture volume. (Photo by Archis Achrekar. Courtesy of Centroid Motion Capture and Motion Analysis Corporation.)*

Inertial capture

Most inertial systems use inertial measurement units (IMUs) containing a combination of gyroscope, magnetometer and accelerometer to measure rotational rates. The digital information comes from miniature inertial sensors, which are placed on key joints and points in the skeleton. The motion data of the inertial sensors is transmitted wirelessly to a computer, where the motion is recorded or viewed. These rotations are then translated to the skeleton in the software.

The benefit of this system is that it does not require line of sight, meaning that actors can wear costumes and do not have to be recorded in a studio. However, there are drawbacks – magnetic fields can interfere and the data is less accurate since it is not about a performer's position in space, but the actor's own movements broken down to their constituent parts relative to only their body.

Figure 1.4 *Inertial mocap – an actor wearing a mocap suit with IMUs. (Image courtesy of Rokoko mocap and Animation Tools.)*

Well-known manufacturers include – Xsens, Noitom and Rokoko. You can use the HTC Vive also to capture motion.

Markerless capture

Markerless systems do not require performers to wear special equipment for tracking. Special computer algorithms are designed to allow the system to analyse optical input and identify human forms, breaking them down into constituent parts for tracking. Markerless

Figure 1.5 *An actor being captured without any markers. (© Qualisys 2021 Markerless tracking with Qualisys motion capture. Model Sten Remmelg.)*

systems tend to use both outline and depth sensors – early adopters used Xbox cameras for capturing, for example. What's exciting about new systems using markerless technology is that it needn't cost much to capture, which is reminiscent of the effect of the advent of cheap consumer priced film and video equipment which drove the independent sectors. Now indie games developers can create budget mocap solutions which will diversify the mocap community and promote innovation. More on this in our final chapter.

Needless to say, the quality and fidelity is not as high but the price is more affordable. Solutions include Qualisys, PS4 and HTC Vive.

A note on the T-pose

You may have seen images of actors in mocap suits standing straight, with legs slightly apart and arms wide stretched out at 90 degrees, and wondered what they are doing. This is called a T-pose and actors are asked to stand in this pose at the beginning and end of every take. It

Figure 1.6 *An actor standing in a T-pose. (Photo by Archis Achrekar. Courtesy of Centroid Motion Capture.)*

is used in order for animators to ensure the system is seeing all of the reflectors and the skeleton is aligned – a rough way of checking the calibration of the system.

There are systems that require less regular actor calibration and occasionally we hear about other poses being used, but the T-pose has become emblematic of mocap, so it's important to get used to it as a requirement for actors on every take.

Motion capture versus performance capture

You may have heard of performance capture. While the terms motion capture and performance capture are generally interchangeable, motion capture implies capturing only the *movement* of head and body but no facial or finger data, nor voice. Championed by directors such as James Cameron, performance capture, aka P-cap, aims to capture as near to the whole performance as possible *and* often includes body, hands, face and voice captured simultaneously. We'll talk more about the difference in the coming chapters.

So, now we've defined how mocap works – though we've only skimmed the surface and there will be more detail to discover in this book – let's just go back to that revelation about the skeleton for a moment. So, if the skeleton is all that is captured, how does what the performers do affect their skeleton? How might they control that? How might they learn how to work with it? Just what is it that is so difficult or challenging about driving a skeleton?

The performer as puppeteer

Even if the actor's skeleton is used to drive a character or avatar that looks nothing like them and that character moves differently from how they usually move and the data can be manipulated by the

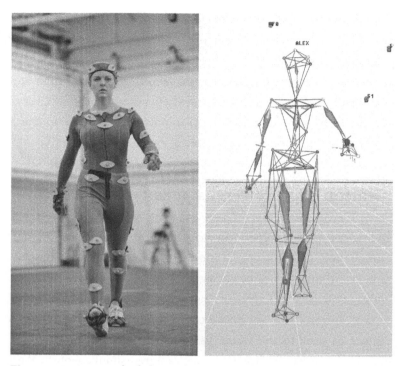

Figure 1.7 *An actor's skeleton drives the animated character. Centroid Motion Capture. (Photo by Archis Achrekar.)*

animator afterwards anyway, the quality of the data is essential. If the actor doesn't create great movement data that drives their character, then the animator might well end up having to do so many corrections that they might as well have not used an actor in the first place.

Motion capture is often used rather than traditional digital animation because it allows the performance to be more life-like and 'believable', plus it is often used in photo-realistic productions such as video games, virtual reality and movies – mostly in stunts, 'digital doubles' and crowd scenes. We will be talking largely in this book about these uses for motion capture, with a focus on video games, since the majority of mocap work is currently in this medium.

The other reason games developers and movie producers use motion capture is cost. It can bring the budget of a game or film down considerably if mocap is used. Think of a modern AAA game title. There are often hours of cutscenes, thousands of moves that make up all the permutations of what the characters might do in gameplay, and all of this has to be animated. Imagine the difference to an animator if the motion capture data which drives the characters is both clear and true to the character and it is created in one go by the actor – it can save them so much time and effort in post-manipulation.

Back to that skeleton, it may also surprise you that you can read performance, tension, breath and minute gestures from the 3D cloud data mentioned above. The performance must be accurate, motivated, truthful, committed and gestural in order to be read clearly. Often the whole of the character's body will be seen in a video game, so the stage actor's understanding of their character's gesture and posture comes into play. An awareness of how the body communicates is very useful, since often in games the player has control of the camera and it may be that they choose to watch the character's performance from a distance or up close. It's then that the skills of an actor used to playing to the cheap seats far away *and* those in the front row come into play. Being truthful to all potential audience perspectives is a tricky skill and one often needed in video games. That's why the medium requires a hybrid of skills – from the gestural, corporeal skills needed on stage to the close, psychological medium and close-up shots from acting for screen.

But it's not as simple as that because, as Stéphane Dalbera points out, 'There is no frame! There is no audience. There is no camera. This is the biggest conceptual shift for the mocap actor.' Not only do you often not know where the player might decide to view the character, very often there is no camera present to play to and there is definitely no audience except for a handful of crew, many of whom are staring at computer screens. Added to that, the performer is usually wearing a Lycra® suit covered in dots instead of a costume and is performing in what looks like a rehearsal space. Instead of a set, the props and furniture are often covered in foam or made out of scaffold bars, wood crates and chicken wire.

And yet, the performer will be expected to create truthful, energized, motivated and committed performances in these alienating conditions. No wonder some actors liken it to playing in black box or in-the-round theatre. This is acting stripped back to the basics and if the character is not embodied believably, it will show immediately.

It may surprise you to hear that, for Stéphane Dalbera, 'walking is one of the most difficult things to do in mocap'. The walk forms the basis for a character and mocap data scrutinizes the walk in detail. We have seen many students crumble when asked simply to walk across a room in character. Why is this? Well, we will talk more about this later in the book, but motion capture is forensic in analysing movement, so tension, lack of flexibility, breath and posture are all exposed in the data.

> When we finished *Lord of the Rings*, I just thought, 'I'm gonna go back to my career as a normal actor. Doing stage and film and TV'. And then Peter Jackson said, 'You wanna play King Kong?' And I thought, 'Man, I'm going to go from a 3 ½ foot ring junkie to a 25 foot gorilla'. This is the end of typecasting as we know it. This is it! You can play anything. Anyone can play anything.
>
> ANDY SERKIS quoted in an article from *Insider Magazine* 13 July 2017: 'After playing Gollum, Andy Serkis has continued to rule motion-capture acting – here's why he loves it'

Well, as we know, Andy Serkis knows his stuff about motion capture, but what he is not telling us here is that you can play anything, *if* you have the ability. And many actors don't have the skills or experience. They lack an understanding of their bodies, they don't have the acting chops, they don't listen to their fellow performers, they don't know how to do the research and preparation to create a strong character and performance. As Gilles Monteil says, 'many actors do not have the tools, teaching or precedents to know how to perform in mocap'.

Don't despair. Don't stop reading. We are here to inspire, educate and inform you and to assure you that if you read this book and act on our recommendations, advice and suggestions, you will be in with a much better chance of getting that break in mocap. It will be challenging, but we hope it will be fun too! Acting for motion capture is an exacting and gruelling business and there is increasing competition as more actors come on stream. However, at the same time, there are more and more opportunities. As the understanding starts to gather that the combination of movement, character and acting skills is crucial, we are starting to see a change in the drama schools of this world who are finally cottoning on to the notion that digital media production is here to stay; that the new acting skills required for voice acting, motion and performance capture, green and LED screen,[4] immersive technologies – VR, AR and MR[5] and volumetric capture[6] need to be taught alongside the traditional stage skills that inspire all of the above.

The irony is not lost on us. Digital media production generally, and motion capture specifically, in their current form have only been around for a few decades, but the skills that are required go back far further than the 130 or so years that screen performance has been around. As Gilles Monteil reminds us: 'Greek theatre was physical, pantomimic and not-text reliant. Much meaning was communicated through the body.' We need to rediscover the corporeal skills we have lost along the way – lost due to religious teaching that the body should be separated from the mind, lost recently due to film's need for psychological truth over the physical, lost because physical theatre and mime have become marginalized in storytelling. This brand-new medium is reminding us of the ancient one of complete acting skills that require the body and mind working in harmony to create truthful, believable and entertaining performances.

Chapter 1 takeaways

History of performance styles	Humans have been performing corporeally for centuries. Religion limited it. Silent movies brought it back. Animation and mocap require performers to use the skills of old in this most contemporary medium.
Digital and virtual production	Mocap has been born out of the reality of digital and virtual production, facilitated by the development of real-time engines and video games. Interactive storytelling has now become mainstream.
Mocap – the technical lowdown	Whether optical, line-of-sight, inertial or markerless mocap, all capture the skeleton, but performance capture also captures the voice and face.
The performer as puppeteer	A first taste of the challenges ahead of using the performer's body to drive the digital skeleton, which in turn puppets the skin of the animated avatar character.

By the end of this book, you'll not only have a clear idea of what motion capture is and what is required of the performer, but also how you might fit into the world of motion capture and what skills and approaches you need to hone to get there! We hope you enjoy exploring this fascinating and innovative medium and that we have some fun on the way.

Notes

1 As told to interviewer Studs Terkel in 1960.

2 https://www.unrealengine.com

3   https://unity.com

4   Green screen and LED screen acting: Technically called a 'chroma key', a
     green (sometimes blue) screen is a flat, evenly lit coloured surface that can
     be easily removed in post-production and replaced with any number of
     visual elements. Like mocap, it requires the actor to use their imagination to
     bring the environment to life. Unlike mocap, the actor is shot on film or
     video, using live-action cameras. LED screens are becoming increasingly
     common (e.g. Disney's *The Mandalorian*) and are similar in concept to
     green screen, but instead replace the monotone background with the display
     of a digitally shot environment, screened live on LED screens behind the
     actors. A confluence of technologies that redefines 'virtual production' and
     means shooting in the desert can be achieved in a suburban studio
     anywhere.

5   Immersive technologies – VR, AR and MR: The word 'immersive' is used to
     describe experiences that completely surround a person to make them feel
     part of an alternative environment. Immersive technologies refer to any
     technologies that digitally extend or replace reality for the user. They come
     in many different varieties, and as such can be used in very different
     contexts. Recent developments in immersive technologies have created new
     opportunities for viewers/consumers/players/audience members to use
     virtual reality (VR), augmented reality (AR), mixed reality (MR), haptics
     and more in gaming, mobile technology and virtual performance – both live
     and recorded – in a fast-evolving arena.

6   Like mocap, volumetric video capture technology is a technique that
     captures and digitizes the performer or object in real-time in 3D using an
     array of cameras set in a studio around a target. However, it uses video
     'live-action' cameras rather than infra-red cameras as outlined in this
     chapter for line-of-sight optical mocap. The captured video of the
     performer/object can be digitized and transferred to the web, mobile, or
     virtual worlds and viewed in 3D. Due to the 3-dimensionality of the process,
     it works well for VR and AR, or any format where the viewer/player has
     agency and has the freedom to move to view a performance from where
     they like.

2

The body

PASCAL LANGDALE

As we have established in our opening chapter, motion capture only records the movement of the skeleton in space. Physical posture and behaviour are the primary modes of communication. The added layers of clothing, speech and facial expressions are not yet present. Physical and behavioural truth in mocap is the pre-eminent focus. The actor needs to ensure they understand their body's own pre-sets and physical history, and what it is communicating to the player/audience in every second that passes. In this chapter we examine how communication works, utilizing and re-imagining the tools gained through actor training. Lecoq's 'neutral mask' and Rudolf Laban's continuums and directions are explored to help us understand our habitual body and how to work truthfully outside our 'casting box'.

Contributors – Oliver Hollis-Leick (creative director, actor, co-founder of The Mocap Vaults, mocap director at Saber Interactive), Richard Dorton (actor, USA casting director, director, mocap teacher for The Mocap Vaults), Gilles Monteil (realization director, animator, movement specialist, Ubisoft Montpellier), Gareth Taylor (actor, games and theatre director, specialist movement teacher for The Mocap Vaults), Paul-William Mawhinney (actor, performance capture tutor at The Mocap Vaults) and America Young (stunts, actor and cinematics director of mocap and voice).

When you're an actor people often ask what you do for a 'proper' job or ask if they might have seen you in something. The most telling question for response however is – 'What *kind* of actor *are* you?' You probably know your answer right away. Did you choose by medium, such as TV, theatre or film? Or did you define yourself by the method you use?

In a profession that has so heavily swung to a reliance on brand, and repeated role types, the idea that the actor could describe themselves as a human chameleon sounds pretentious at best and economic suicide at worst.

What if we told you that it's possible to change your physicality so totally, your movement, gesture and posture, rhythm and tempo, that someone who knew you well could not tell who you were?

Motion capture provides the possibility of such transformation that previous generations would envy. And previous generations *would* envy such a privilege. Because the desire for physical transformation is something that has existed for as long as storytelling, even if in the West the connection between mind and body has been generally discouraged for hundreds of years.

Much of the suspicion of consciously trained physical behaviour and gesture comes from a rejection of European theatre that became increasingly stylized from the late seventeenth century onwards. At its most extreme these styles dictated that an actor should script their gesture, similar to a musical score, matching the words. This type of show-and-tell has its heritage from a time when pantomime and dumbshow were the predominant form. Shakespeare's Hamlet complains of it when he tells the players, 'Nor do not saw the air too much with your hand, thus' (*Hamlet* Act 3 Sc.2).

The ascendance of silent movies demanded the actors skilled in pantomime: replacing words with signals and symbolic gestures and exaggerating physical behaviour for broad comedy. These made stars out of Charlie Chaplin, Buster Keaton and Harold Lloyd. Talkies made this kind of mime redundant. Instead, it was the fusion of Freudian psychology with Stanislavski's early work that confined the perception of acting technique to a style that was suited primarily to the screen.

It is still the case that a great number of actors and teachers who come from this established 'method' approach insist that physicality can't be changed too far from the actor's natural range. They believe only 'inside-out' approaches that focus on psychological logic result in truthful performances.

However, the 1960s saw a new focus on physicality in theatre outside the United States, and some of these schools have persisted, mostly drawing on the work of:

- Étienne Decroux (1898–1991): First exponent of 'corporeal mime' – mime of illusion of everyday activities, always performed with intention.

- Marcel Marceau (1923–2007): Inspired by Chaplin, he was a student of Decroux and his peers. Marcel described mime as 'The Art of Silence', and his work can be seen as a blend of Chaplin and Japanese Kabuki.

- Jacques Lecoq (1921–1999): Coming from a sport and physical education background, Lecoq's notable approach was for actors to develop their own technique by learning what didn't work. A key part of his training is mask work.

- Augusto Boal (1931–2009): Founder of 'Theatre of the

Oppressed'. 'Image theatre' was a technique he developed where actors moved other actors into physical positions to express relationships and emotion.

Other useful physical systems:

- Rudolf Laban (1879–1958): Famous for inventing a system of movement analysis and codification, by defining movement intent and structure.
- Moshé Pinchas Feldenkrais (1904–1984): Developed a method of somatic education, teaching the student how to move with greater ease and efficiency.
- Frederick Matthias Alexander (1869–1955): Created a system of physical awareness through effortless practice, removing redundant stress and effort, and countering imposed physical heritage.

We are now at a point in our understanding of human behaviour that provides the best argument for techniques that result in embodied performances. What do we mean by 'embodied'? For the purposes of this book we have settled on this interpretation:

The most complete physical, psychological and emotional transformation an actor can make, to the point that even someone who knows them would not recognize them except for their visual features.

Up until recently this would be an impossible ideal if not only for the extraordinary cost of prosthetic makeup and body suits that would be required to change visual features. This changed with the arrival and advancing quality of the medium. Motion capture, as we have established, only records the movement of the skeleton in space. No clothing, hairstyle or skin colour is registered. Outside of physical idiosyncrasies such as disability, injury and physical heritage there are a few physical qualities that *can* affect skeletal movement; gender can, due to the degree of mechanical difference, and muscular structure and body fat due to its influence on the skeleton.

Where movement comes from

Imagine this: You are standing in your new accommodation. The floor is cluttered with opened boxes, the contents of which are in various stages of being organized. You decide you need some water from the kitchen, which is on the opposite side of the room. Your friend, who is helping you unpack, has asked you your opinion on a thorny subject about their future. You pick your way through the clutter, talking to your friend as you cross the room and enter the kitchen.

What you have just done is an extraordinary feat of multiple processes between mind and body.

The moment you decided you needed a glass of water from the kitchen, your brain was already plotting a course through the clutter, mirror neurons firing pre-movement tests between your brain and the muscles you will need to set off and walk.[1] The moment before you spoke, the image of what you were describing and wanting to communicate was divided into words and gestures, one complementing the other – each adding information it lacked alone. Moreover, the important words in each sentence were underlined by gestural and verbal emphasis (paralinguistic). Word and gesture are tied within a predictable time frame.[2] You do this to pursue your multiple objectives in the most efficient way possible, assessing the potential cost to the 'body budget', the amount of reserved energy available.[3]

Movement is a result of the need to achieve multiple goals, matched with appropriate management of complexity and effort, qualified by your personal psychology and physical state.

Or, to put it another way: You just crossed an obstacle course talking to a friend without thinking about each word and gesture, unconsciously performing innumerable complex physical calculations, whilst also navigating the emotional needs of the relationship. This ability may be unique to all humans, but the way *you* do all this, is unique to you.

Physical heritage. Your life is in how you move

Do you remember when you first heard a recording of your own voice, or watched yourself on the screen? Were you surprised by how you sounded or how you looked? There is a parallel here with your current perception of your own physicality.

Often, if you ask an established motion capture artist when the penny dropped about the nature of motion capture, they will recall a moment of physical betrayal. A moment when what they thought they were communicating with their body was completely different from the reality as shown in the bones of their digital skeleton. For Gareth Taylor (teacher and experienced mocap actor) it was when working on a commercial. He was performing as a cocktail barman. He was told his actions were too slow, and were still too slow when *he* thought he was going fast. For myself it was on the mocap stage in the obvious untruth in the lack of weight of a shoebox in which there was a gun. Equally it can be as simple as watching the playback of your skeleton as it walks across the volume. All the heritage of your sports or dance activities, compensation for old and current injuries, the genetic inheritance of bone and muscle arrangement, the psychology of your overriding attitude to life itself, can be seen in a walk. Gilles Monteil rightfully points out that a walk is one of the hardest things for a novice mocap actor to master, because it is so totally exposing of your own personal physical heritage. Decroux devoted a large portion of his training to the walk. It can be considered your physical fingerprint.

It is this that conservative method actors will say cannot be altered without destroying truthfulness, that your own life and physicality are *the* truth from which you must always work. All characters, in this way, become a variation on your own normal physical behavioural range.

This *does* make sense in an increasingly brand reliant industry, where archetypes are fulfilled anew by each generation of film actors. However, it doesn't make sense in an industry that relies on the actor

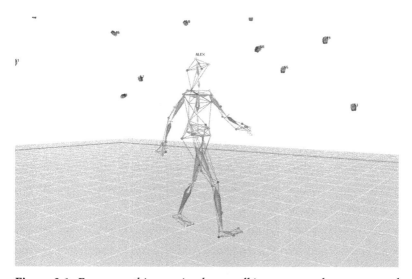

Figure 2.1 *Even something as simple as walking can reveal your personal physical heritage; not the character's. (Image by Centroid Motion Capture.)*

to be able to embody a great variety of archetypes, characters and creatures, with a physical truth that can pass the digital test of mocap.

What is an aspiring actor meant to do then, to be free from the telltale signs of their own physical heritage and embody the physicality of another?

Decroux advocated a system of training that can be hard to appreciate in today's culture of quick video tutorials and intensive courses. He believed that the actor should move from silence to speaking over a period of *thirty years*; the first five of these years to be spent in exercising the body to train muscle memory on quality and musical density rather than movement or musculature. The idea was to train the body as a pianist would train their muscle memory and control, to play at the highest level. It's an oft quoted statement that it takes 10,000 hours to master anything. With multiple areas to master, Decroux recognized that the craft of acting is a life's study.

Kinesthesia, proprioception and mind–body connection

Kinesthesia is the sense of your body's *movement* in space. Proprioception is the sense of your body's *position* in space, as well as the sense of balance. To be able to identify your own physical heritage and embody a different physicality improvised in the moment, you need to train both, whilst increasing the free interrelationship between the mind and the body.

Can you become a child, a drunk, a drunk forty years your senior? Can you become a troll, a dragon, a soldier, a dragon soldier? Can you do this while grieving the death of your closest companion, or celebrating a victory against impossible odds? The ideal I'm driving at here is to become an actor who can do these things and make them interesting and believably compelling with little to no preparation, all specific to the story character. All in the same day if necessary. Moreover, you need to know that what you intend to communicate to the player is indeed being communicated, as the character. There should be no walking gait, timing or movement that doesn't belong to the character in the environment and in the scene; not a single 'leak' of your own physical fingerprint.

Motion capture is a place of infinite possibility and creation. For the same reason, mocap can also be the most demanding of all the acting mediums. It is important to note that TV and film also have challenges such as green screen and virtual production and continuity – and this is where the skills required align with mocap performance. TV and film also have large numbers of people watching and adjusting hair and makeup, making intimate scenes even more challenging. Such physical contact is rare in motion capture as the markers can disappear from sight of the camera, and even 'migrate' to the other actor's body. It can take an age to separate whose marker belongs to whom when processing the data. With those caveats, here's a comparison breakdown of the different media in their most common incarnations.

Voice work

- Character and narrative: Carried by audio only. Physicality is insinuated by vocal expression and sound effects.
- Skills: Good sight-reading skills, rather than memorizing a script. Wide variety of consistent vocal tones and accents. Using distance between your mouth and the microphone, turning the head slightly off mic on plosives (Ps, Bs) and some fricatives (Fs). Strong vocal technique (especially for game

VO), that can be relied on, and recover quickly from high volume work.

Theatre

- Character and narrative: Carried by the script, physicality, voice and visual mise-en-scène. Physicality is adjusted to the scale of the theatre, larger theatres also meaning that audience members further from the stage also need to be served by the performance.

- Technical skills include: Memorizing a script; good vocal range and strength; physical expression of a character; ability to 'cheat' the body open to the audience even in theatre-in-the-round; hit pre-set positions for lighting and other effects.

TV

- Character and narrative: Carried largely by the face, the script, the voice, and mise-en-scène in a physical set. Physicality is normally the performer's own, framed in increasing closeness for the sake of one or two cameras.

- Technical skills include: Ability to mute physicality according to the lens and final product frame size (TV); hit pre-set positions for lighting and camera; ability to work out of sequence in small increments repeated multiple times.

Film

- Character and narrative: Carried largely by the mise-en-scène, the actor's face, the script and the voice, normally on a real set. Physicality is normally the performer's own, or close to it, framed in increasing closeness for the sake of a single camera.

- Technical skills include: Ability to mute physicality according to the frame size and final product frame size (big screen); hit pre-set positions for lighting and camera; ability to work out of sequence in small increments repeated multiple times.

Motion capture

- Character and narrative: Carried by the physicality, script, voice and virtual mise-en-scène. The set and all elements of environment and costume are virtual, and physical props are over-scaled proxies. Physicality is adjusted to the camera position and frame if known or played in '360 degrees' to a player who can be watching in any position at any distance. The virtual environment must be imagined along with costume, proxy props must be endowed with their virtual versions, all adjusted to context to tell the story nonverbally.

- Technical skills include: Ability to quickly memorize a linear or interactive script, good vocal range and strength, physical expression of a character or creature similar to or very different from the actor's physicality; hit pre-set full body positions to match the start and end of a sequence; perform repeated differing actions as a result of player multiple choice; work with physical constraints due to animation rules; work in physical discomfort wearing a headcam and tight Lycra® mocap suit; create characters at extremely short notice; collaborate with multiple leading team members whilst protecting and advocating for your craft; physically enact another performer's vocal track; accept that even the most skilled and complex contribution may simply be described as 'mocap'.

Just in case you are unfamiliar with the term, mise-en-scène is the visual elements that go into telling a story through set design, props, costume, lighting and actor blocking and direction.

Whereas some films may rely on green screen or virtual sets, the majority don't. Some theatres may be immersive and therefore have a variable audience position, but most don't. However, mocap routinely requires skills that are only sometimes used in other media, as well as more skills that are particular to animation.

Falsehood in performance is magnified by motion capture

Your centre of balance is shown in the organization of your skeleton. Pretending that something has weight may be convincing in real life when the underlying skeleton is hidden by flesh and clothing. A well-mimed effort can create extraordinary illusions assisted by the audience suspending its disbelief. In contrast, mocap is never fooled because there is no other information other than the skeleton to cover up or mediate a falsehood. Any assistance is created by the mise-en-scène and the animator later on. Age, physical type, facial appearance and clothing are built on top of the data you have provided in the mocap volume and dropped into a totally manufactured environment. If your performance data contains something revealing its artifice, it must be corrected by the animator, or if unnoticed may still become obvious to a player and pull them out of the experience, maybe even turn it into a gif that will haunt the internet for years!

The animator will be looking at the reference video too, using their judgement on how to enhance what may have been lost in the data cleaning (see Chapter 4, 'Mocap Is an Animated Medium'). If you have delivered performance that appears false, it may well persist through the pipeline. As a quick and last resort, the smoke and mirrors of effects or masking action with camera position may even be employed. It can all be done 'in post', but your job is to reduce the time and resources spent correcting what you could have done. The animation team has enough to do correcting and enhancing what you couldn't have done.

For example, if you are faking the weight of an object, the captured skeleton will show how you are compensating to make the illusion rather than making a physical counterbalance to a real weight. Depending on its level of importance this may need to be corrected. The same is true of performances when the psychology and physicality are not connected, or do not match that of the character. If you are playing a troll, it is not enough that you embody weight and mass you do not have, you must also be psychologically 'troll' and manifest that psychology in every moment and movement that you are physically present in the scene. If you are indicating weight by stamping your feet, and 'phoning it in', mocap will reveal your falsehood and you will pose a costly problem for the animators.

Figure 2.2 *In both the images above the actor has been asked to pull against a weight. (Photos by Archis Achrekar. Courtesy of Centroid Motion Capture.)*

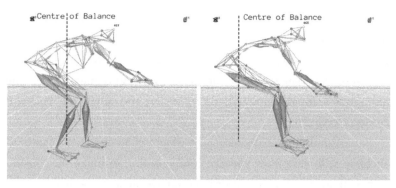

Figure 2.3 *The point cloud data reveals any illusion by highlighting the skeleton's centre of balance. (Photos by Archis Achrekar. Courtesy of Centroid Motion Capture.)*

Figure 2.4 *The uncropped reference picture. Mocap is never fooled. If you are faking the weight of an object, the skeleton will show how you are compensating to make the illusion, rather than making a counter balance to a real weight. (Photos by Archis Achrekar. Courtesy of Centroid Motion Capture.)*

Commit as much as if you were hired in a lead role on a major movie or a major stage show. And commit with a whole body or 'embodied' performance. If you don't, you will only disappoint yourself, and you may not be asked back.

Train your mind–body connection

There are a variety of ways you can improve your mind–body connection. Almost any sport or physical exercise can improve your balance, control and sense of your body's position in space – mostly proprioception. Many established mocap talents have a background in gymnastics. The most well known may be Terry Notary, who is best known for his work in the mocap suit and as a movement choreographer for films franchises such as *Planet of the Apes* and the *Avengers Marvel* series. He started gymnastics at eight years old. But you can also add the contributors to this book, Gareth Taylor and Oliver Hollis-Leick. A dance background is shared by both myself and Richard Dorton, and America Young has a background in stunts. These physical backgrounds can be easily adapted and integrated with acting. One of the best mocap actors I worked with trained in clowning and martial arts. No one physical training and background is the answer, it's the adaptation of useful skills that is.

However, any system of restrictive physical training has an inherent risk of reducing the range and spontaneity of physicality and movement; moreover, it will leave its mark on how you use your body. Dancers may find it hard to play heavy or physically awkward characters, gymnasts may find it hard to be chaotic. Of the systems that are out there, yoga and Pilates are regularly cited as the most useful. This is because although they are highly formalized movement and exercise systems, they train both proprioceptive and kinesthetic skills. They also focus on integrating the breath, something considered of great importance by every performer interviewed for this book.

How to train

Make no mistake. This chapter cannot tell you how to be a master nonverbal storyteller. It is a matter of practice and training. It is a highly rewarding lifelong pursuit. The following exercises are therefore designed to give an indication of the territory you must explore and the magnitude of the task at hand: Train your kinesthetic sense and proprioception and understand how and why you move, and how and why others move too.

Look around you

The first is quite simple and yet requires you to change the likely habit of a lifetime. If you're reading this book, notice how you are sitting, the arrangement of your body, and what that might tell an observer about you and your relationship to the book. What if you change the point of view of the observer? If you're in a public space look up for ten minutes or more and watch how people walk, talk, gesture, or just sit. Every moment presents a chance to observe other types of physicality and the stories you derive from them, and understand your own.

All the actors interviewed for this book copy people in everyday life. Unobtrusively embodying someone's walk (see below) or noting interesting postures and gestures should become second nature. It doesn't have to be a human; you can also embody your cat or your dog. Your success and comfort in being able to do this can be improved with the following exercises.

An exercise in Laban

Laban is often associated with the codification of dance movements; however, Laban classified the different qualities of movement to allow anyone interested in movement to explore physical expression.

According to Laban, all movement contains up to four 'Effort Factors' or 'Qualities': Weight, Space, Time and Flow. Each of these has its extremes. Strong and light Weight, direct and indirect Space, sustained and sudden Time, and free and bound Flow. The various combinations of between two and four of these mediate physical movement, causing changes to your movement, the way you walk or sit, gesture or interact with objects. It can change your internal mental state.

It is apparent then that this is an ideal tool to understand and embody different physicalities from your own. And like all physical systems, it's best learned by *doing*, not reading or talking about it.

Before you can run, you must first learn to walk. And before you walk you must train your mind–body connection and increase your facility to allow the body to lead your movement. You have likely spent much of your life thinking your body was the slave to the mind and the will. As you will discover if you delve further into Laban and embodiment, the body keeps the score. The body can tell you how you really feel and can ambush you when you ignore it. It carries the effects of your upbringing, your habits, traumas and your psychological outlook. If you want to be able to physically transform, it starts with a better attitude and relationship to your body.

An exercise in body-led movement

Clear a space from all objects at any level that you might hit with any part of your body in an area at least twice the size of your full reach from the centre in any direction. Take this seriously, because you want to be physically aware of what space you have and feel free to use it. Also, as with any physical exercises, don't do them if you have an issue you'd be wise to consult with a doctor or physiotherapist about first.

Now, lie on the floor and close your eyes. Take two or three deep breaths. Wait.

At some point you will most likely want to stretch. This desire to stretch is a useful starting point for this exercise, as it is the most familiar way your body tells you how you want to move. Your task is to move *as your body wants to move.*

Slowly at first, allow one movement to lead to another and another and notice when you start to think about it. Let those thoughts go and focus again on moving according to how your body feels. Let the desire to move appear to you on its own. Do not try to push, direct or make nice shapes or dance. You are not dancing. In fact, if you direct your movement with your mind you are more likely to injure yourself. Listening to your body moment to moment means you can work safely around injuries because the body won't choose to do anything to make it worse. If done properly you will go through contortions that stretch and strengthen what *needs to be stretched and strengthened to exactly the right degree.* You will enter into a sort of physical meditation that allows you to move fast or slow at the right time and introduce a great range of types of movement at different speeds and qualities.

Starting Laban this way means that the next step – of categorization – is more likely to be a result of experience, rather than the more arbitrary translation of a linguistic description. Do this every day for at least fifteen minutes and you will notice changes to your strength and flexibility within a couple of weeks. It is better to do this before looking for courses in Laban for actors.

An exercise in walking

As we noted above, Gilles Monteil says, 'Walking is one of the most difficult things to ask an actor to do.' He notes that as soon as you pay attention even to your own walk – the individual nature of the swing of the hands, angle of foot placement, centre of weight and position of head – the ease of your habitual walk starts to break. Follow this exercise in the steps we recommend. Do not be tempted to watch your videos first!

1   Get someone you are comfortable with to video you or use a tripod. Record walking directly towards and away from the camera. Walk in a circle around the camera as it follows you one way and then the other. Have the camera follow you held at the same level as your hips, from behind and in front. All these videos should have your full body in view. Try not to focus on, or change, your walk. Recite a speech or poem, or count back from 100 to give your mind some distraction if necessary.

2   *Before watching the videos*, go for a walk and deliberately focus on the following areas. It may help to record the following list a few times on one track and listen to it as you walk. Ensure there is enough time between the areas of focus for you to actually focus!

- Is your weight more forward or back?

- Where is the walk leading from?

- How are your feet striking the floor?

- How are you swinging or kicking your foot forward with each step?

- How long is your step? How wide from the central line?

- How do your hips move? How does this affect your shoulders and back?

- How does each arm swing? How does each hand move or how is it held?

- How is the head held and where does your gaze normally focus on?

It's quite likely you will have to do this a few times before you can relax enough to ensure the observation doesn't affect what you are observing. Be interested and curious. If necessary, change something in your walk to find out what you go back to naturally.

3   Notate, in your own way, all the elements of the walk established by the questions above and any others you have identified. Now you can look back at the video and see how closely and how accurately you have analysed your own walk. Approach yourself with curiosity, not with criticism. If you find you are judging your walk, stop the exercise. This is no place to start comparing yourself to an 'ideal' or trying to emulate an ideal you have in mind. Your body is your body. Learn from and respect it. Get to know yourself better so eventually you can embody other people better. Until you can look at your own physicality with intelligent curiosity you had better work longer on the Laban exercise above.

4   In the outside world follow and observe other people walking. Pick one aspect of their walk you want to mimic. A hand flap, a foot fall. Copy it as best you can and then *ask how that makes you feel*. This is crucial to establishing a connection between your mind and your body. Once you have explored this, make a new movement, an adaptation or addition to your walk. In public. Because there's nothing like walking in a different way in public to help keep you being truthful and proportionate. You won't be tempted to exaggerate or lose the intention behind the walk.

An exercise in silhouettes

We cannot help but make judgements on appearances. These may be corrected over time, but we wouldn't have costume and hair and makeup departments for contemporary dramas if appearance signified nothing. We also wouldn't see archetypes consistently associated with body shapes. A character actor understands archetypes as a broad culturally curated collection of physical and behavioural characteristics associated with repeated narrative roles. These should be used not as an end point but as a launching point to create a unique version of one archetype or blend of more. Without this creative development, archetypes will descend into their often-mistaken cousin, the stereotype. And you don't want that.

Body shapes have always been used by animators and actors to signal archetypes. Think of the folk tales or graphic novels in your culture. You will soon see physical themes repeated by many of the heroes and villains. The reason is that shapes find their power in shapes found in nature. Our 'old' brain, the amygdala, is wired to respond with fight, flight or freeze when we see certain shapes that signify danger in nature, and other shapes are associated with displays of strength or aggression.

This exercise is best done with a partner, ideally wearing a mask or even a sheer veil you can see through (Decroux used this method). An alternative is to set up a light that can throw your shadow against a black wall, positioned so the shadow is near to your own proportions.

Look at the images in Figures 2.5 to 2.7. Triangles signify strength; irregular angular shapes, danger; a mix of curves and triangles signifies a healthy, integrated strength.

Using these images as inspiration, find a standing pose that you believe creates the impressions associated with these shapes. Experiment mixing shapes between the top part of your body and the bottom. What happens if an arm is crooked but the rest is curved? Your aim is to find the distillation of a hero, a soldier or a monster archetype. If you are lucky enough to be working with a partner, ask for feedback and adjustment, then *ask to be looked at from behind*. In

Figure 2.5 *Triangles are associated with strength and aggressive display. (Artwork by Eden Bø Dower.)*

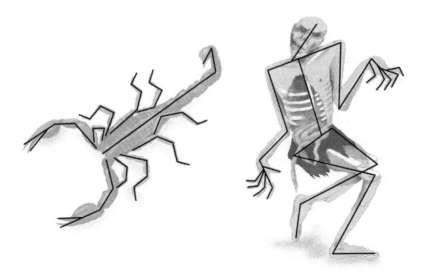

Figure 2.6 *Irregular angles are associated with danger. (Artwork by Eden Bø Dower.)*

Figure 2.7 *Angles and curves are associated with healthy and integrated strength. (Artwork by Eden Bø Dower.)*

many games this is the view the player will have of the hero/lead character for hours of gameplay. The vital question then is does your body's pose and its silhouette instantly communicate your archetype from behind? As in the previous exercise, ask yourself, *How does it make me feel?* Don't forget to breathe!

The letter exercise

Change your body to match the shape of the following capital letters, in turn, as you walk. C, Y, I and Z. You will find that the letter shapes correlate to the shapes in the previous exercise but don't try to find just triangles and curves.

Next, walk around, interact with objects, sit, stand, always trying to maintain a greater or lesser manifestation of the shape described by the letter. Don't only focus on the physical changes, limitations and freedoms the shapes offer, but also focus on what it does to your breath. Again: How does it make you feel?

This last question is one that has already cropped up regularly but is often overlooked. It is a vital part of establishing a link between the physical and psychological, the playground and guide of all the best embodied performances. For example, 'C' shapes might make you feel sad, 'Y' shapes, strong . . . What do 'I' and 'Z' make you feel?

An exercise in animal study

Silhouettes drawn from nature are an inspiration for shape but are not in movement. Animal study takes this further and, according to Oliver Hollis-Leick, this is by far the best and fastest way to dramatically and believably shift your physicality in a short period of time. He cannot stress how useful this has been to him over the years, both in mocap and on stage (film also applies).

> Animals have strong physicalities and they embody so many characters we meet in daily life – the anxious rat, the bullish gorilla, the lazy bear, the playful dog, the aloof cat. When used in the right way, animal study is like a super-weapon.
>
> OLIVER HOLLIS-LEICK

Choose three different animals. Spend maybe twenty minutes observing them in their natural habitat using online videos or documentaries. Zoos are not necessarily the best location, as many of the animals show behaviours defined by their restricted surroundings. A tiger pacing backward and forward in an enclosure that is used to many square miles of territory will not provide the best material. There may be some benefit from observing *some* animals confined in zoos, but generally the larger the animal the more diminished the returns. The kind of nature documentary made famous by David Attenborough is normally much more useful.

After you have spent twenty minutes with each animal, choose one of them and then stick to it. Spend a further day trying to get into that animal's world.

> Don't project onto it, study it as though you have never seen it before. Look at the minute detail, the weight shifting, the curves, the angles, the way it interacts with its environment, its own species and other species around it. See the animal. Study it until you start to sense its unique perfume, its unique qualities. When you have that, start to become that animal. The devil is in the detail.
>
> OLIVER HOLLIS-LEICK

And so it is. Using your newfound sense of weight shift, tempo, and energy, now include the curves and angles of the animal's body. Go back and forth between the source material and your own exploration until you feel you can 'drop in and out' of the animal's physicality. Remember to put yourself into different states – how do you relax, play, or present stress and threat?

Next is to make that connection with the human. What if a human had the physical and mental attributes of your animal? Don't try to impose your idea of what that would be like. Instead, start walking around the room, sitting, standing, performing mundane tasks – as bold and big as you like at first ... this is not the final product. By doing this, as in other physical 'rehearsals', it's OK to be too big in order to then keep the essence of what you discover as you make your behaviour more subtle. Go from bold to stage level, to filmic close up and back again. Eventually find the scale that you will be happy to test out in public. And yes, go out to a public place and interact, you'll quickly see where that scale of believability is.

Richard Dorton can draw on a range of previously worked on archetypes as starting points for quick character work. In the same way, Oliver has a collection of animals. He recommends working on a new animal each week. We will integrate animal study with character work in the next chapter, but as with all these exercises, animal work should expand and be kept in mind in everyday life. As Oliver says:

> Another thing you can do is start to see people on TV or (eventually) in person and use your imagination to sense their animal. Don't start telling people their animal because that isn't always appreciated! Know it for yourself ... I wish you the best of luck with this exercise. It transformed my approach to acting and I love it deeply.
>
> OLIVER HOLLIS-LEICK

Chapter 2 takeaways

Train	Hone your muscle memory, and senses of proprioception and kinesthesia, for effortless and complete physical control.
Learn about you	Transcend your own physical heritage so it doesn't show up in your character.
Nonverbal storytelling	Through real-life observation and practice, learn how to tell the dramatic story you want to the audience/player.
Commit	Put your efforts into truthfully embodying the character or creature – physically, emotionally and psychologically.

Notes

1   *The Brain's Sense of Movement*; Alain Berthoz (2000, Harvard University Press).

2   *Hand and Mind: What Gestures Reveal about Thought*; David McNeill (1996, University of Chicago Press).

3   *How Emotions Are Made: The Secret Life of the Brain*; Prof. Lisa Feldman Barrett PhD (2017, Macmillan).

3

Imaginary environments

PASCAL LANGDALE

You are asked to creep through a dense rainforest in perpetual rain, carrying a sword, expecting to be ambushed by a stealthy carnivore. However, you are, in reality, in a sterile empty motion capture volume, with over-cranked air conditioning, wearing a Lycra® mocap suit holding a stick enveloped in pink foam. The extreme level of detailed imagination required to bridge the enormous gap between fiction and reality can often paralyse actors.

This chapter draws from experience of actual shoots, highlights regular traps and hazards and provides examples of techniques to meet the challenges of bringing the environment to life through your performance. Environment is not just a question of the external world. It's every part of the imagined world that has a physical effect enough to be part of nonverbal storytelling.

Contributors – Gilles Monteil (realization director, animator, movement specialist, Ubisoft Montpellier), America Young (stunts, actor and cinematics director of mocap and voice) and Gareth Taylor (actor, games and theatre director, specialist movement teacher for The Mocap Vaults).

Humans are constantly interacting with objects and the environment around them. Our senses provide us with the information we need to have control over the physical world as we find it, or react to the environment as it affects us. In film, TV and even theatre, actors either have the real environment or near proxies to help put them in the world of the narrative. In the mocap volume, furniture is replaced by wooden and wire framed constructions, or tape on the floor. If at all. Weather and other environmental conditions must be entirely imagined by the actor, on top of all the other considerations of bringing a character to life. Imagination therefore, is the foundation and muscle that must be worked on until the skills become second nature. This skill we will call nonverbal storytelling, rather than physical acting, which can have overtones of a certain style of demonstrative acting.

We recommend reading the second chapter of Michael Chekhov's *To the Actor: On the Technique of Acting*, which retains one of the most complete lists of imagination exercises in a single book. One of the most important things Chekhov teaches is that imagining something by visualizing it, as you might see it in a film or photograph, is not the only way to create fictional realities to live in. Many actors believe a filmic recreation is what is being asked for when asked something such as, 'Imagine yourself in a forest'. The first instinct is often to attempt to imagine every tree, sucking up the available bandwidth that should be dedicated to acting. The goal, then, is to find how your imagination is triggered, to place you in an imaginary forest, without the need to recreate every leaf. For this you need to consider all your senses, and discover which ones reliably drop you into the world you are imagining.

You can start by simply asking yourself these five sense questions, digging deeper beyond one of the ten questions familiar to method actors, 'Where am I?'

- What do I see?
- What do I hear?
- What do I smell?
- What do I touch/feel?
- What do I taste?

For example:

I *see* ... an open landscape of grassy savannah, grass thigh high, pushed like a Mexican wave by gusts of light wind. I see puffy clouds slowly moving across a clear blue sky. There is a herd of deer in the mid-distance peacefully moving through the grass, feeding as they go.

I *hear* ... the wind in my ears, the swish of the grass, there are meadow birds somewhere I cannot see.

I s*mell* ... the damp earth, fire smoke.

I *touch/feel* ... my thick boots in the soft earth, the heavy pack straps cutting into my shoulders, the wind in my hair and in my eyes, my aching feet.

I *taste* ... the metallic taste of hunger.

Even if it may not seem necessary to know what the soundscape is like, or what you can taste or smell, it is just as well to ask yourself, because it may be the trigger that brings you into the imaginary world. You will likely find two or three senses that are your go-to.

These questions are the starting point for the character to move within. Once the world is defined, the remaining questions are about stakes, objectives and threats. These questions are questions that will be mediated by the environment you have now established. Once you believe your existence in the environment, your character will reveal itself by how they pursue their objectives within that environment and context. You won't feel the need to 'show' anything. As an actor, you want this interaction between character and environment to be automatic and symbiotic.

Don't pantomime or lose touch with drama

If you don't have faith in your own suspension of disbelief, you will be tempted to 'show' the environment, and this is the realm of pantomime. On the other hand, you may recreate real life so much that the effect is to be undramatic at best and boring at worst. After all, life takes place over a timescale that even games can't compete with and drama is focused on 'The moment when'. In terms of heightened behaviour, between pantomime and real life, is corporeal mime. Both mimes are 'illusion mime', but corporeal mime is the revealing of an invisible world with realistic intent. Pantomime is a heightening of the importance of the physical world, where it is the object or the environment that becomes the story: grasping a doorknob is done in a way that brings the door into focus, normally for comedy. In comparison, in real life, you are walking through unremarkable doors on unremarkable days amongst many other days. In mocap, corporeal mime is the ideal form, as the door becomes a way of serving an objective/intention in the drama of 'The Moment When ...'. You are deliberately telling a story. If you remember this, you will avoid the curse of over-acting and 'indicating' everything or underacting and failing as a compelling storyteller. Instead, find a way to be in the environment, in the story, and banish the emptiness of the capture volume.

The actor's job: nonverbal storytelling

The empty space of the motion capture stage demands reacting and interacting with and within an imagined world.

It has often struck me how lucky I was to be seen for many commercials in my early career. Many of these were for European adverts where little or nothing was said, catering as they often did for multiple countries speaking different languages. As a result I was often asked to imagine complex environments, unlikely events and scenarios, and bring them to life in a small casting room. 'You're walking through the store and a trapdoor opens in the floor, you

Figure 3.1 *Empty space to be filled by your imagination. (Photo by Archis Achrekar. Courtesy of Centroid Motion Capture.)*

fall through and land in a party taking place in a ball pit.' You get the idea.

The truth is, that even the most mundane of actions in motion capture have to carry character and story, manifested in the skeleton. Even approaching a table can be done in a myriad of ways, depending on character, previous circumstances, current stakes, what's on the table or what should be on the table, and the environment – cold, hot, foul smelling and so on.

Gilles Monteil remarks that he often comes across experienced actors who cannot adequately nonverbally tell a story. As each medium requires different skills or delivery of performance, actors are often physically trapped and too reliant on the words, and Gilles ends up on many occasions doing the motion capture later himself. America Young notes: 'If [actors] come from TV rather than theatre they are used to hitting the mark, living in their heads and giving physically still reads that will come off as flat in mocap.'

The consensus is that actors experienced in theatre, particularly classical theatre, have an edge when it comes to scaling their physicality to the needs of the volume. But it's not just a question of scale. It's a question of physical storytelling.

> Usually the problem is being uncomfortable or unfamiliar with how to express the story through the body.
>
> AMERICA YOUNG

Some actors have an innate ability, but as Gareth Taylor points out, he's a great singer in his head, but when Gareth sings it's far from his imagined skill. To be a good singer, you must take steps to learn how to use your voice and handle a song. To be a good nonverbal storyteller you must learn how to use your body and handle a dramatic arc.

Neutral mask work has a long heritage going back at least to Charles Dullin in the 1920s. Now, it is the closest you can get to

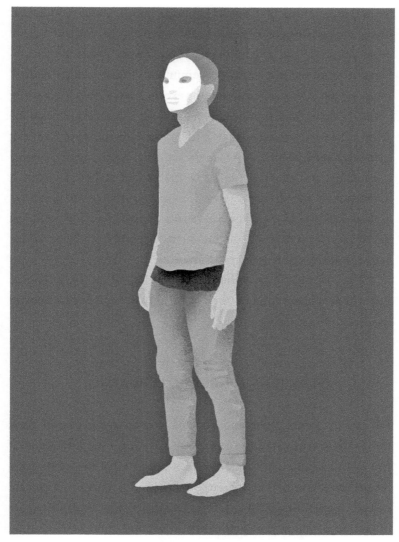

Figure 3.2 *Mask is highly recommended to train nonverbal storytelling skills. (Artwork by Eden Bø Dower.)*

motion capture without being in a mocap studio. Gareth recommends taking a course wherever possible. By removing the voice and facial expressions available to communicate, mask work forces the actor to focus on what the whole body is communicating. Finding a 'neutral' state, one that communicates nothing except possibility, is the starting point. He notes the attitude of the mask work is similar to that of the actor – one of curiosity and play. With practice, and hours of watching each other, the student begins to understand the economy of nonverbal storytelling, and the best timing of events and actions to make it interesting – the dramatic arc. Even an improvisation based on looking for food in a kitchen can have a dramatic arc, told with just the right amount of interesting moments inspired from being in that world, timed to create a dramatic progress.

With or without this training it's useful to look at simple techniques that will help bring you into the imagined world and release enough bandwidth to act within it.

Rehearse, rehearse, rehearse . . .

We are not talking here about formally dedicated rehearsal time; this is about rehearsing the action you have just been told about. If you have already asked questions and seen whatever supporting images they have, you now need to rehearse. For example, if you are asked to walk through a forest, trees marked only by multiple crosses of tape on the floor, you should walk in and out of those trees, using the sense questions mentioned above. Even if the director wants you to make a straight path, rehearse the environment all the same. Also, the simple question of, 'Am I walking to something or away from something?' can define the intention that must be shown in the movement.

Figure 3.3 *Tape on the floor is a guide to how you move through the world you have imagined. Walk through and around the tape to reinforce your experience. (Photo by Archis Achrekar. Courtesy of Centroid Motion Capture.)*

If you are asked to do something apparently mundane and everyday, the rule applies no less. Just because you get into a car every day, doesn't mean that getting into the car in the volume will be a cinch. For a start you may have to semi-mime a door, grabbing hold of a metal bar that has been established as the correct position. Then your car may just be a wooden seat with an upright back. Before they shoot, go over the action of getting into the car a few times. In the first run, focus on the environment; in the next run, focus on the mechanical activities; in the last run, focus on character. Eventually you will be working on all these aspects simultaneously without effort. You'll see many experienced mocap actors walking through sequences of physical activities talking to themselves, describing what they are doing and why, while they are doing it. '... I grab the handle automatically, while looking around for a potential attack ...' It may seem strange, but when you deliver three competitively viable takes in a row, no-one will question your approach. Sometimes this step-by-step description can include the director, framed as a desire for confirmation – this ensures you are both on the same page, but also gives a less hands-on director the opportunity to add what may be missing.

The job in the volume

One of the mantras of mask storytelling is 'What's next?' – there can't be a more suitable approach to mocap storytelling, where game characters are always pushing forward into the next action.

GARETH TAYLOR

So, knowing the environment is your job, but how much that shows in the final performance is up to the animation team. You may be walking through deep snow in the cinematic, but if the locomotions don't have a collection of walks under different snow conditions, physically enacting walking through deep snow won't be needed (locomotions will be examined in more depth in Chapter 6). So much of storytelling in game is about performing physical actions to achieve an objective in environments and circumstances that are new to the character. One of the frequent oversights Gareth warns against is failing to realize that every cinematic is surrounded by a much greater proportion of the character moving through the game world pursuing an objective. Even more than that, competition is inherent in the fabric of ludic (game) storytelling. Whether you are competing against a zombie horde, or hacking a megacorp server, your objective is to beat the obstacles and win, under whatever terms the game has set.

As this is the reason behind the game, your performance may come second place. It is vital to be prepared to show the effect of the environment on the character. Prepare to be asked to 'do less', 'dial it back' or 'be more generic'. All that work you did may just not be wanted, but your job is to provide what the animation team needs. Getting the balance between what you can manifest and what they have in mind is a negotiation of options they may be surprised to learn that they have.

Imaginary environment example exercise 1

Go take a walk. Whilst you are walking take time to:

1   Make sense observations as listed above.

2   Change one or more of the conditions sensed. For instance: 'I feel the cold on my face' can turn into 'I feel the heat on my face'; 'I can hear children playing' can turn into 'I can hear monsters calling to each other'. Play and allow that to have an effect on you. Find out what senses best trigger the suspension of your own disbelief.

3   Choose an opposite environmental effect to reality and go into a coffee shop or grocery store and make a purchase. Turn a warm and friendly shop into a noisy cold one where everyone is staring at you. It will have to be so believable that people will explain your behaviour with a logical assumption.

Imaginary environment example exercise 2

An adaptation of the 'Many Uses of a Brick' exercise:

1   Place a small object, about the size of a water bottle, in the centre of the room. From the side of the room, walk to the

object, pick it up and return to the side of the room. Put it back.

2   Repeat the exercise, changing the environment. Hot, cold, raining, humid, windy, typhoon, tornado . . . you get the idea. Use the sense questions to drop you into the chosen environment.

3   Repeat the exercise but this time changing the nature of the object within a range of extremes. Its quality varies from something light to something heavy; its value from trash to rare treasure; its effect from something dangerous to something beneficial.

4   Add weather. Repeat the exercise.

5   Finally, add immediacy to the objective. Repeat to yourself why the objective is important now: 'I need this vaccine to save the world before it decays', or 'I need to move this bomb before it goes off, to save the city' etc. . . . Add weather, and go get the object.

Imaginary environment example exercise 3

This exercise expands the idea of physical external environmental stimuli, to include internal and narrative stimuli to tell a nonverbal story.

Sit in a room and smile. At the end of two minutes you have to storm out of the door. How does that story go from smile to rage in two minutes *without speech*? Why do you end up storming out the door and what was the dramatic arc that got you there? What was the trigger that changed the mood?

- For your first attempts you can use something external to trigger the change – a text message or a picture on the wall.

- For the more advanced version, choose an internal trigger – a sudden thought or recollection, memory or image.

Repeat with variations:

1 Change your state: hungry, thirsty, nauseous, tired etc. . . .

2 Change the environment: hot, cold, humid, threatening, blissful, unfamiliar.

3 Change the story by choosing two new physical positions/ actions at the start and the end.

4 Change the final activity: Perhaps you end up dancing, or crying, laughing or collapsing?

Summary

In this chapter we established that a strong imagination is key to bridging the gap between the empty space of the mocap volume and the finally realized virtual world your character will inhabit. We have shown how you can use a range of senses to pull yourself into the imagined environment, and that your job is not to demonstrate, nor to be dull, but to tell the story of your character in that environment in an engaging way. We call this nonverbal storytelling. Too important to overlook, it is nevertheless possible that the animation team may not want to see more than a generic pass. It may be that you have a natural skill, but imagination is a muscle, and can be trained and improved by exercising it through mask work and imagination exercises. What other media provide for free, a mocap actor must imagine. Being able to not only believably create a character but also the world around them is an exceptional feat, and if you succeed you can count yourself among a rare number of exceptional actors.

Chapter 3 takeaways

Train your imagination	It's a muscle. It improves and strengthens with practice. Read *To the Actor: On the Technique of Acting* by Michael Chekhov.
Use your senses	Don't imagine every leaf on every tree, use your senses to evoke and pull you into the imaginary environment.
Find the drama	Develop your sense of drama in nonverbal storytelling: mask work is recommended.
Corporeal mime	Every second is a chance to physically tell the story so make the invisible world physically visible with clear intentions. For example, if you turn your head to look at something, know what demanded your attention.

4

Mocap is an animated medium

JOHN DOWER

The truism that actors need to understand how their performance is being interpreted through the medium in which they are working applies equally to mocap. If film acting obeys rules defined by the camera view and subsequent editing and theatre acting requires adaptation to widely viewed live performance, it follows that mocap acting must adapt to the needs of animation. The actor in motion capture needs to understand they are working in an *animated* medium. The performance is planned, overseen and finally shaped and manipulated by the animator. We will also look at the video game pipeline and how a video game is developed over time. In this chapter we will gain an insight into what the animator is looking for from the performer, how their animation can be inspired and improved by the actor and how to ride the ups and downs of video game development.

Contributors – Goran Milić (head of facial at Goodbye Kansas), Gilles Monteil (realization director, animator, movement specialist at Ubisoft Montpellier) and Ralph Palmer (head of animation at Rebellion).

An actor habituated to live performance on stage may find the sterility of the mocap studio disconcerting. Even a film actor's performance relies on a starting point of 'what you see is what you get' being the limited foundation for all the post production that may be possible. Therefore, the actor works in a costume, most often in an environment physically like the story world, and may benefit from seeing their performance in rushes or playback. Plus, they will have had a sense of the story world since they were most likely to be shooting in a film set that approximated it or at least wearing a costume that helped to make them feel like the character they were playing. The mocap actor who has none of that will be performing in an abstracted space, finding themselves playing to imaginary screen partners, quite possibly having neither a clear idea of where the camera will be nor of how their character will end up looking. Their character and performance are placed through data into the hands of the animator, who wizard-like can change any aspect of the original performance and the world around it.

How does this happen? What is the process their data goes through before ending up shiny and new as their on-screen avatar? And why is there such a difference in animation quality and style from motion captured data? We will look at this and more, but before we do let's just define just what animation actually is.

What is animation?

Animation is the process in which objects or figures are manipulated to appear as moving images. The word stems from the Latin word meaning 'a bestowing of life'. An animator's primary job is to make us believe that the character in front of us is alive, thinking and conscious. In the more rudimentary animation, for example early hand-drawn or cell-painted 2D, this meant that the character had to keep moving in every frame in order to make up for the lack of detail on the face or body, which might break the suspension of disbelief. Likewise, even when it comes to fully realized HD digital characters, it remains the case that constant movement is crucial. Live action film makers can take the HD or film camera for granted and know that every breath, muscle movement, blood flow under the skin, movement and quality of the eyes, will transmit a sense of life going on. A close up of an actor shot on film can sustain prolonged audience scrutiny – particularly if the actor has great technique and can transmit their inner psychology into their face – even if the actor is not moving, merely thinking. I could watch an actor like Mark Rylance just *thinking* about the telephone directory on camera and find it interesting! Animators must recreate all of this to make it appear their characters are conscious and thinking.

As we've established, motion capture captures motion, not the nuances mentioned above. Some years ago, I cast a very good film actor in a game and was pulled aside by the animation producer to look at her mocapped performance, reacting to the main character. What had seemed in the volume to be sensitive and alert listening, was rendered lifeless once in animation. There simply wasn't enough physically happening in the data to read in the animation. She appeared dead for several moments! This is where the previous exercises we have looked at for the body and our emphasis on bringing the body to life through breath come into focus. This death-by-stillness is what animators have to avoid, and an understanding of this for performers and performance directors is essential.

Because motion capture is an animated medium, the actor has to appreciate what the animator needs to help bestow their shared character with life.

The mocap data pipeline

What follows will be an explanation as to how the mocap data and animation pipeline works. I've tried to keep it as simple as possible, but I'm aware it may seem complex for some. Since this is a new medium and there have been few books, online tutorials, courses etc. to try to explain it to non-animators, this may seem overly thorough to some of you. However, we believe that those performers and directors who have a good understanding of the technology will be at an advantage – just as those who understand how film and television are brought to the screen are at an advantage in their preparation, working on set and in post-production.

We've outlined the technology in the introduction and underlined that it's the skeleton that we are trying to capture, but we need a little qualification there, particularly when it applies to Lycra® suits for optical and inertial capture. Markers are fixed to the suit and, though the material is figure hugging, it will move in relation to the actor's skin – muscle and body fat will move the markers in relation to the joints. Also, the markers need to be seen by the motion capture cameras. If they can't be seen, the gaps in marker information will need to be made up.

The mocap technology is not as precise as we might want it to be and this has a knock-on effect as the data moves down the pipeline. We've heard that even the best mocap studios' pipelines can get only 95 per cent accuracy of what the actor does. This can go down to considerably less in lower budget studios. Particularly when working with optical/line-of-sight mocap, it is important for performers to appreciate the system and make sure their performance and gestures are not unnecessarily obscuring or occluding markers and thus preventing the cameras from seeing them. Although in some cases it may be desired, it is worth noting that crossing the arms can cause this, as can standing near to or against opaque surfaces or lying on the floor.

Often the data reflects these imperfections, so the first stage is to send it to technicians to fix. Once the markers have been reconstructed during the 'clean-up' process and anomalies in the data are corrected, technicians then 'solve' the skeleton into the markers. There are on average around 60–65 markers on a mocap suit used to approximate the human skeleton.

Once the skeleton is defined and solved, then it is 'retargeted' onto the character. Animators often look for actors who have the same size and proportions as the digital character, or as near as is possible, because this makes the retargeting process more streamlined. This applies particularly to human characters, which make up the majority of mocap characters. However, it may well be that a character has different proportions from the actor e.g. an orc, an ogre or an ape. We will outline later in the book the challenges involved in playing a character with different physical characteristics and qualities from our own.

Just to recap, for those want to get some clarity into this process, the motion capture data pipeline can be roughly broken down to five steps:

1   Acquisition

- Actors in suits – optical, or inertial or even markerless.
- Props.
- Vehicles.

Figure 4.1 *There are on average around 60–65 markers on a mocap suit used to approximate the human skeleton. (Photo by Archis Achrekar. Courtesy of Centroid Motion Capture.)*

- Reference video.
- Helmet-mounted cameras (HMC) (if facial capture is being used).
- Clean audio (if performance capture).
- Fingers/gloves (if finger data is being captured).

2 Cleaning

- Reconstructing motion capture camera data.
- Filling gaps in markers that could not be seen.
- Smoothing jittery data.

3 Solving

- Deriving translations and rotation for skeleton joints.
- Fitting the skeleton into the marker cloud.
- Analysing and tracking a face from HMC footage (more on this later).

4 Retargeting

- Reinterpreting a performance onto a different character/ creature.

5 Animation

- Taking the performance to a different place.
- Exaggerating a performance.
- Creating something entirely different from what the actor did.
- Making the performance suitable for a video game.
- Creating cycles.
- Enforcing poses.
- Re-timing – speeding up/slowing down.

The animator interprets

Once the data has been acquired, this is when the interpretation begins. Even at the cleaning stage, what's noise and what's human has to be sifted through. Up to this point it's been an objective approach. This is where the first subjective moments come in. The animator must decide what was important about the performance. The character data is now in an animation application such as Motion Builder[1] or a real-time engine like Unreal or Unity.

It's now that the animator can position the cameras – which can be created at this point, or maybe the *virtual camera* data, which was recorded at the time of shooting (more on this later), is used. It may be that once you have the cameras defined, the animator will need to go back to the mocap data and re-solve, knowing what the camera sees. At this point, in any case, there is often a lot of editing done. Despite the mocap pipeline being a flexible and iterative process, if at any stage the animator makes a significant decision or compromise, that may have to be carried all the way through the pipeline.

Other contemporary computer-generated animation processes, for example machine learning,[2] are 'top-down'. Once the computer has learnt what Al Pacino should look like in his forties (e.g. from the 2020 Netflix film *The Irishman*), it will apply that rule to every frame. But you can't go back to the source like in mocap – instead, what you see is what you get.

Capturing the facial performance

So, we've talked about the body being captured via the skeleton and then the data being put into the animation pipeline, but what about the face? How does that technology work? Does it go through a similar process?

Goran Milić, head of facial capture at Goodbye Kansas, Sweden describes the process thus: 'The goal is to collect your facial performance.' Facial capture is not quite the mostly automatic and responsive process we've described for mocap. You might have seen videos of actors with markers glued to their face, or with dots drawn on. This is the optical method of capture. According to Milić: 'Optical has some benefits – no head-mounted camera is needed, actors can perform close together and are only restricted by the size of the volume' (which is smaller because the data is harder to capture given the complexity of the face) – 'eight to twelve metres square max. Another benefit is technical – the data is easier to stabilise'. This is partly because, with optical markers, depth can be determined more easily – though multi-view HMCs can also determine depth – making

Figure 4.2 *'For animators, everyone would pick an HMC' (Goran Milić). (Photo by Archis Achrekar. Courtesy of Centroid Motion Capture and Faceware Technologies.)*

the point cloud in space clearer. But then he adds: 'Last time I used an optical system was 2007.' Why? And what does he use instead?

'For animators, everyone would pick an HMC, because you get a great reference of the facial performance at all times' (Goran Milić). The head-mounted camera (HMC) is currently the predominant method of facial capture. At the high-end of mocap animation, gone are the days of glassy skin, dull eyes and rubbery lips. Players and audiences expect faces that can show emotion, that express what the actor is thinking, that have been made to feel as real as possible. In games, whereas lifeless objects can look photoreal, anything that has life is in danger of looking unconvincing in comparison.

The HMCs capture more detail, getting more from the eyes for example, which is crucial for close ups. Besides, according to Milić there are two other disadvantages to optical facial capture: 'If you have some running or fighting or whatever, they get sweaty, markers fall off. Plus, there is more work afterwards when you use optical.' It is unlikely a HMC will be used during action sequences, where the camera and helmet can move, break or simply impede performance, and very rarely during stunts. In those cases, the animator will have to resort to either optical or, more likely, use as reference whatever has been picked up by the studio camera, also known as 'witness or reference cameras', as described later.

The HMC records video that creates digital data which tracks the facial movements of the actor. When an actor is engaged for a facial capture job, often they will be brought in to do a 'range of motion' (ROM) set, the purpose of which is to train the tracking software to recognize what your unique face and lips are doing using machine learning, active appearance modelling (AAM)[3] or other methods.

'Most of the products for tracking use similar principles. They track the features of the face – lips, nose bridge, eyes and brows. The

Figure 4.3 *You will likely be asked to perform a facial 'range of motion' (ROM) which will include extreme facial expressions of fundamental emotions, eye movements and lip shapes. (Actor and photos by Pascal Langdale.)*

results are not always great. Some places lack the details – the cheeks, for example' (Goran Milić). The ROM trains the analysis software, but data might still be missing. So, what then? It sounds like an inexact science. What do the experts do if data is missing? 'Without the ROM, it's still possible to track the data 1:1 perfectly, but it will take more time and it'll be harder to batch process multiple shots' (Goran Milić).

The ROM teaches the system how the actor's face moves, using a system called the *facial action coding system* (FACS) to categorize what the facial muscles are doing. FACS is designed to differentiate human facial movements and expressions.[4] Certain collections of FACS positions are associated with expressions that convey emotions. Other ROM poses are about eyes and lips. Once an actor has gone through these different expressions and the facial capture system has recorded them, 'blend shapes' are created. 'Blend shapes creation is related to facial modellers and riggers. It's usually a long and manual process of either hand sculpting or a scan polish of the basic FACS shapes, building the rig and adding in-between shapes for better transitions' (Goran Milić). FACS is a way to describe any facial pose. Combinations will give basic emotions, and more complex combinations create more complex emotions.

It may be that at this time the actor's head is recorded in 3D in a process called photogrammetry (this is a process of capturing digital images then going through photogrammetric processing, which allows the generation of 2D or 3D digital models of the object as an end product[5]) or the data might be transferred onto another digital character much in the same way that has been previously described in the process of animation for the body.

A proportion of the facial animation is procedural – which means it happens automatically – and some is done later by animators. The ratios vary, depending on the quality of the system and on how much the actor's performance communicates clearly. What is important to understand is this:

> If the actor's face is not communicating that facial expression clearly, or if the director or animation supervisor are not happy with the performance, it will have to be altered in animation or re-shot. Actors can perform however they like, and the performance can be transferred to the character 1:1 but if the director doesn't like it, it may need lots of work in animation to make it good.
>
> GORAN MILIĆ

This may be hard to hear for actors used to their performances being definitive, nuanced and very much theirs, but as we have said all along, creating a motion or performance captured performance takes a team to complete.

There are other situations that can complicate facial capture which are outside of the performer's control. Faces shift due to gravitational effects and movement – skin will stretch and slide, there

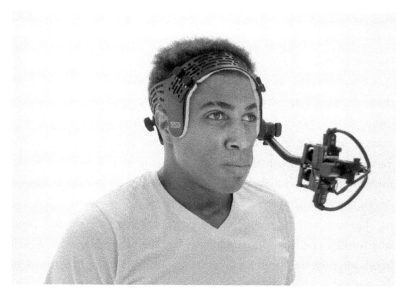

Figure 4.4 *Facecam Premium (two cameras). (Courtesy of Standard Deviation. Actor: Philip 'Fury' Wainwright.)*

will be tremors in the muscles, especially during more physical scenes. The HMC is sitting on skin that itself is sliding across the skull. Here the tracking returns the nearest match interpolated between the closest match it has in its data set. If this doesn't look right, the animator will have to interpret the performance and correct it to the right facial expression.

Like body mocap, there are a variety of capture solutions. At time of writing, a company acquisition reduced the number of high-end facial capture and Analysis SaaS (Software as a Service) providers down to one. There are several budget solutions. For example, if you have heard about the iPhone X's capability as a facial capture device, you may wonder, what's the difference from a facial animator? 'It depends what your goal is. In a situation you need everything to be in Sync' budget facial capture 'doesn't work for film where a large volume of data is required as they are not gen-locked [synchronised using timecode]. For personal and budget projects – they work fine' (Goran Milić).

Head-mounted cameras are coming in many shapes and sizes these days with up to four cameras on board to give a more three-dimensional view for the data. However, even with every pixel as a marker, and even if we have scan-based profile building and multi-view cameras for depth, there is often still a big difference between the mobility and expressivity of the human compared with the animated character. According to Goran Milić, there are 'many reasons: the rig, lighting and hair need to be perfect. Perfect cinematics need fine tuning. For example, the pucker up, the funnelling nose which bends slightly, the tongue movement – all need to be fine tuned in animation'.

The reason that facial capture is so complex is that: 'Everyone is a facial supervisor. Everyone is watching [other] faces all the time. If something is off, people notice that. Everything needs to be good quality, every stage' (Goran Milić).

We will talk more later about the reality of working with head-mounted cameras. They may work well for animators but are often a challenge for actors who have to put up with wearing them for hours, with distracting cameras and lights right in front of the face. Facial capture technology may be getting better, but the performer will often feel as though their quality of experience and comfort is not the priority. As we said at the outset, motion capture animation came out of technical development and innovation – with performers often feeling as though they came as an afterthought. I have been arguing for the input of the performer and the director to be appreciated more, ever since getting into this medium. Facial capture technology must improve in the future the comfort of the performer, which in turn will improve their performance.

The eye of the animator

OK, so we have established that facial capture is complicated and that animators are needed to sort out the nuance and sometimes interpret, but what about the body? Isn't that a more automatic process? Joints and bones obey universal rules and are therefore clearer to read than an eye twitch or how the tongue moves, right? We've established that motion capture technology is a complex, computer-heavy affair and that the processes are lengthy and painstaking. The process has been known to be disparagingly described as 'digital makeup' by well-known filmmakers (more on this later). Just what is the role of the animator in mocap? Doesn't the tech mostly take care of itself?

According to some of the leading animators working in mocap, there are some interesting answers to that question. To ex-Disney animator Ralph Palmer, it's about bringing the data to life. He says '[mocap] needs the eye of an artist. Film is based on emulsion, it's sloppy, it's always moving, but it feels alive. My job is to take that data and try to make it look like the emulsion. To make it feel like film.' To Gilles Monteil, what's important is the player's experience. His interest is:

> to try to push the boundaries of animation for games. I am not so interested in creating high fidelity animations. I am not interested in total control. If you do a great animation and you see it three times in a row it's boring ... It's more important for the player to have a good experience. However, the actor's performance is crucial ... if the raw data is of bad quality, I will never succeed in getting a final good result. It's layers of quality and each of them are important [so capture performance, editing and after that real time animation techniques – all need to be top notch] even if at the end, the player's experience is paramount.
>
> GILLES MONTEIL

Ralph Palmer also talks about the artistry involved, using the example of Disney: 'Snow White was rotoscoped. But filmed and then printed on animation paper, then traced and then the animator made changes to the design. It's still different from the original. They take key frames, and then the artist fills in the gaps.'

From a director's point of view, having an animator there makes everything so much clearer because then you get an idea of how they see the important elements of the performance in the studio, how it will move through the pipeline and how it will read on the character at the end. If there is a separate performance director then they collaborate with the animator, but if the animator is also the director it means there is only one person doing the job on their own and the animator is even more important.

One key concept to remind ourselves of is that the animator's job is to give the impression that the animated character is bestowed with life. They are always fighting the danger that the character might appear to be dead! So, the animator is trying to make stillness dynamic, to give a sense of internal consciousness with whatever tools they have at their disposal. And it's not just the quality of the animation – it's also the lighting: 'If the animation is amazing but the lighting is bad then the eyes will look dead' (Goran Milić). Goran adds 'Eyes and fingers are the two things that bring the most life to a character.' There has been much work done over the last decades to bring the detail into eyes and fingers. Like dots on the face, reflectors or markers on fingers are also complex to capture. Indeed, most mocap studios will charge considerably more per second for finger data. These days there are companies, e.g. StretchSense,[6] who specialize in finger and hand capture. In the latest *Last of Us* instalment we see a mocapped character playing a guitar, and the detail is both impressive and uncannily real.

Figure 4.5 *StretchSense gloves are dedicated to finger capture. (Stretch Sense, 2021.)*

When it comes to games, there is an added issue – the player is the most important element and the animation has to serve them. Gilles Monteil explains:

> What was super obvious coming from acting, is that it was more like improvisation and you needed to improvise according to the rules set up by the game. The player of a game is like an improv actor – so you have to create a volume of actions that needs to react to change of decisions. The player will still have a linear experience and they will want to get a proper response to their inputs. This is another layer on motion capture editing, sometimes we need to know that an animation is captured to be blended with another one or interrupted at any moment. All the game is a spontaneous story.

So here we have an animator who prioritizes the experience of the player, and how they will play the game and respond to the characters, over beautiful animation. It is clear that when actors are performing in mocap for a game they need to take into account how the player will experience playing with their character – if they are the main character – or how they will be as NPCs (non-player characters). We are talking about a medium that is radically different in form from stage, film or TV and we must always be conceptually aware that, in games, it is the player who is in control and we must always take account of the interactive nature of the relationship with that player. 'The point is the player can destroy the performance because he or she is one of the actors. In addition, all the NPCs have to be reactive, have to look intelligent, unique and appealing as characters-actors' (Gilles Monteil). It was clear in talking to Gilles that he saw his job as conceptual, interpretive and highly creative.

The role of the animator is to create characters we believe in, performances we are engaged in, and particularly in reference to games, to encourage us to interact with. Animators are involved in every stage of the motion capture process and this starts long before actors turn up at the studio. They will have worked with the games designers, writers, environment team and performance director – if there is one. Animators may also direct mocap shoots themselves. Whoever is directing may well be working from character designs and artwork given to them by the design team. They may even have completed rough but complex versions of the scenes known as pre-visualization, previs or *pre-viz*, which they want to try to replicate in the volume. Whatever, this leads to a factor that makes working in motion capture challenging – the animator will have a clear idea of what they want, which is not about the performer personally. Film, television and stage is usually about you and the director helping to create a character, with the actor at the centre. Sometimes in mocap it can feel as though the performer is there to service a character that is already either partially or fully formed. The extent to which animators and performance directors appreciate this challenge posed to their actors is dealt with in the following chapters, but it is essential that the actor appreciates what the animator is looking for since their performance is essentially a part – a crucial part, but nonetheless still only a part – of the animation pipeline.

The animator relationship with the actor

It's important to put the perspective of the animator in context. As performers and directors, it's our job to have empathy and understanding of our collaborators' perspective. When motion capture began to become a serious animation medium, there was significant resistance from animators. Gilles Monteil puts it into context for us:

> I remember animators saying that motion capture would steal their job. I think it was the same for drawing artists when photography appeared. Today we can see that a good photo uses composition based on painting research and history and that illustrators are using photos as material. The same thing is happening with motion capture actors who need to understand the movement rules and animators who are using motion capture data to create their own animations.

Because of this point, and the fact that mocap is still developing as a medium, it's also important to point out that, for many animators, using skilled actors is a relatively new experience. In the early days, many animators would act the parts themselves. It shouldn't surprise you to learn that animators are usually skilled observers of human movement, gesture and emotion. Many have mirrors on their workstations, so they can copy an expression they have created to show an emotion. Many will use themselves as models for reference.

Up until a few years ago, motion capture performers were a rarified and expert group of stunt, combat and physical performers, who complained of being seen as 'flesh puppets' by animators who had little idea of how to motivate or direct them. When I first worked in mocap as a director, there was suspicion that I would 'dominate' the capture process and tell animators what to do, maybe also show up their shortcomings as directors. As soon as they realized that I was there as a collaborator it became much easier for us to become greater than the sum of our collective parts.

Things have moved on and animators are really beginning to gain experience and appreciation for what actors – and directors – can bring to the table, but the tendencies from the early days do persist occasionally. This is not to put you off – there is still much to stimulate and challenge the actor in mocap and, as we will consistently argue, the skills required are arguably more exacting than any other medium. However, it is essential to thoroughly understand the animator's perspective. That way, when you come to the studio, you will be able to contribute to their vision of the character.

The difference between performance and motion capture in animation

As you've seen from the chapter so far, capturing a performance is pretty complex. So, if it's possible to capture it all at once (performance capture) why doesn't it happen all the time? Doesn't it make the animated performance better? As is often the case in the animation world, the answer often comes down to budget; plus, not all mocapped animation has much facial animation or voice (e.g. NPCs – non-player characters in games). Good facial animation is generally an expensive component of a budget. Mocap body capture is generally faster than full performance capture, cheaper to run and does not require a sound studio if voice is not involved. In fact, often voices are recorded before and played back in the mocap volume for actors to perform to. Acting to pre-recorded audio is a real skill and one we have found students often find very challenging. It's not so common to find actors who are good and experienced at both voice *and* mocap and since you can often earn significantly more per hour recording voice, these are often seen as different parts of the process. This is particularly true if you think of movie actors who lend their recognizable voices to games. They are less likely to want to come onto a mocap stage where they have to wear an unflattering Lycra® suit and work hard to try to create a corporeal performance that their screen acting abilities might not support them in excelling in.

So, what happens instead? The constituent parts of the process are frequently split up; body being shot separately to face, with voice being recorded at the same time as face, or separately, and sometimes every part being shot separately *and* sometimes even the top half of the face being captured at a different time from the bottom half! In these cases, the bottom half is for lip-sync and the top is mostly about eyes and brows. As you'll understand, this disjointed combination approach is sometimes referred to as creating 'the Frankenstein effect'.

For someone used to full performance capture, Goran Milić is unequivocal – there is 'so much more work. I hate it'. However, for most games with modest budgets, performance capture is too expensive and, in any case, is not useful except in cinematic scenes. Some actors specialize in mocap performance and some in voice. A few bring them all together and get to do performance capture, but only if those hiring them are convinced they will create a great whole performance – with expressive body, face *and* voice. It's an animated medium and all elements of a performance need to be dramatically, gesturally and emotionally clear.

We appreciate that this all sounds complex but we hope that, as you read further chapters, it will all start to make sense as you start to see it in the context of a sophisticated and technically demanding performance medium.

Digital makeup versus augmented animation

So, you've been in the mocap studio aka 'the volume' or you've done your stuff in an inertial suit, you've left the experts to do their thing and finally the finished animation ends up on a screen. How much of your performance is left once the data has gone through the pipeline? How much of the commitment, effort and talent it took to give that performance makes it onto the screen?

The truth is, it varies. In 2011 while making *Tintin* Steven Spielberg said of mocap: 'I like to think of it as digital makeup, not augmented animation. It's basically the actual performance of the actual actor, and what you're simply experiencing is makeup.'[7] It caused a controversy in the mocap world that angered many animators and technicians because, as you'll have seen from the process described above, there is a lot going on in the post process once the actor has gone home.

I am always looking at the actor's performance and using the video reference to get the exact intention, because with the different processes applied on the captured data, some of it will be erased. The goal of the animator will be to retrieve the original intention but not always by copying it but (for good animators) to enhance it. You need to push readability of movement and dynamism, something that an actor will have difficulty to do during the capture. Also, for an important cinematic scene, you can't have something acceptable straight out from mocap ... contacts [with props and environment] eye retargeting, timing, synchronisation . . . all of that will be retouched and rearranged.

GILLES MONTEIL

This is not always because the performance was not good enough. Sometimes it's proved difficult to solve the data and retarget it onto the character. Sometimes the mocap data has proved too difficult to use. This is the case of the well-publicized footage of Benedict Cumberbatch playing Smaug in *The Hobbit*, where the voice was used, the facial capture was used as reference, but not the body performance – which was entirely created by an animator.

However, for much of the time, the performance helps create great animation. Remember – your job is to help the animator, and we hope this book will help you to appreciate what the animator needs from the performer. The more you understand about the requirements of the process and the more you can put yourself in the mind of the animator, the more useful your performance will be. That way, more of what you give as a performance will make it into the animated character.

What animators are looking for in an actor

So, what is the animator looking for in the actor? 'Some technicians will watch the point cloud, some will watch real-time' (the real-time playback of the digital character transposed onto the skeleton). 'I always watch the actor' (Ralph Palmer). This is reassuring and brings us back to the core of the process – truthful physical performance – so it's good to hear an animator watching where that performance originates! Ralph again: 'The actor can see their character and play them. They can see themselves from outside and the really good ones can make it look as if it is happening for the first time in their life.'

Again, this should measure any actor whose aim is to create truthful performances that connect with an audience.

What about technical or physical characteristics? This depends on the role. Talking to animators, for a generic mocap actor with range for use as several characters in a game, animators might look for an athletic type with a uniform looking walk. They are trying to rule out physical traits that pop out so they can be used for multiple characters. Often, actor height and size are crucial since they will be driving a digital character the same size in the game or film scene. Physical characteristics that are not symmetrical can be unhelpful, since they will be noticeable on all the characters the actor plays.

We have worked with students who are surprised to hear about physical tics they were unaware of when we look at how their 'movement heritage' has affected their walk. It's important to remember that you are not playing you – you are playing a character – and that the animator and director will have a clear idea of how that character moves and acts. Your skeleton needs to communicate that.

What if you are playing the background character or NPC in a game? How do you bring that character alive without direct and dramatic motivation and still make your performance useful to the animator? 'If you are playing a baker, *be* a baker. You have to love baking to be a baker. Good news is – there is no subtext! Be the happy baker or grumpy lorry driver. If you are a painter, just paint' (Ralph Palmer).

There is, having said all this, a sense that in animation the voice is more important than the body. It may be that the developer may not know what money will be allocated to a scene, so the safety of having an excellent voice and script (both cheaper than facial animation) makes sense. The reality is that a voice actor can often earn in two hours what a body performer earns in a day. Though outlined in the reasons above as a practical issue, as we discussed in the introduction it has as much to do with the modern world's focus on text and dialogue over physical performance. We believe this will change as corporeal performance becomes more understood and appreciated, but it will also change as animation becomes more nuanced with advances in the definition and detail in digital production.

What you can expect from the shoot

Finally, what can you expect from a mocap shoot? We've talked about working in a 'volume' rather than a stage or studio. We mentioned the T-pose, which can take some getting used to as it is a requirement to hit it before 'action' and before 'cut' on every take. There are also likely to be various cameras around. 'Witness' or 'reference' video cameras will be there, either on tripods or operated so that animators have the reference video we mentioned earlier in this chapter, to refer to later. There may also be a virtual camera, which allows the operator to see the real-time characters in the digital environment, which we discuss in more detail later.

There will be no special lighting since that will be done digitally later. There will be no costumes or makeup for the same reasons. Props and staging will look different from what you are used to and will largely be see through to facilitate line of sight. The on-set technicians will be responsible for logging all the props into the system so they can be recalled and multi-purposed. There may well be a sound recordist if dialogue is being recorded and there will be numerous mocap technicians with possibly an assistant director to support the director and animator. Crews are generally smaller than in stage and screen and sometimes your only audience is a team of technicians glued to computer screens!

A word on schedules and timeframes. This can vary, but generally a game's production schedule is very different from that of a film. It can be more like a relentless ebb and flow as 'vertical slices' of gameplay are produced as proof of concepts for the publisher, and various levels of the game are made. This means that several mocap shoots that may number a few days or weeks over several years are common.

> The design for 'The Division' changed many times. There were five different animation directors – all different in styles. In the development phase we shot a lot of data. It was experimental, not committed. We have a test phase, then when validated we cast for the characters . . . though we might have to re-do and maybe replace the actor. We are constantly shifting which means you want to commit as late as possible. Once you commit with actors you go quicker.
>
> GILLES MONTEIL

I'm currently working on a game with a day's shoot every two months, likely to be spread over eighteen months. As you can imagine, for the actors to keep their focus on their character over this time, it is a challenge. Plus, as a director I have a fear that they might not be available for the next shoot, which would either necessitate waiting for them or recasting – neither of which is ideal.

We hope we've given you a sense of how the animation process works and how animators think in this chapter. It's a technical and complex process, but we view it as an important one to understand. Performers and directors who have both insight and knowledge tend to be able to deliver better and more usable performance data in the studio, plus they are generally better collaborators since they understand the wider picture.

Chapter 4 takeaways

What is our job in an animated medium?	We have to understand the needs of the animator to create characters that appear to be bestowed with life.
The mocap pipeline	We outline the process as: acquisition, cleaning, solving, retargeting and finally finished animation.
Capturing facial performance	Facial capture is probably the most complex and expensive part of the technology and requires truthful and dynamic performances.
The eye of the animator	Despite the technological complexity of the pipeline, there is a surprising amount of interpretation and artistry involved in creating great animation from mocap.
The animators' relationship with the actor	Many animators are not used to working with actors. Understanding the process, and your role, will help you understand and collaborate with the animator.
The difference between motion capture and performance capture in animation	Animators use different processes and combinations of capture to create performances, from combining multiple parts of a performance to capturing a single actor's total performance in one go in performance capture. In contrast, mocap generally means no facial capture.
Digital makeup versus augmented animation	Animators point at the reality of the mocap pipeline, as involving much more creative input than just 'makeup'.
What animators are looking for in an actor	The technical and physical characteristics necessary for doing the job from the animator's perspective, the relationship between voice and body capture, and how physical traits affect performance whether lead roles or NPCs.
The shoot	More cameras than crew, more variation in who is directing you, see through furniture, sets and proxy stand-in props and drawn out and sporadic schedules.

Notes

1 https://en.wikipedia.org/wiki/Autodesk_MotionBuilder

2 Machine learning (ML) is the study of computer algorithms that improve automatically through experience. It is seen as a subset of artificial intelligence (AI).

3 An active appearance model is a computer vision algorithm for matching a statistical model of object shape and appearance to a new image. Computer vision is an interdisciplinary scientific field that deals with how computers can gain high-level understanding from digital images or videos. A statistical model is a mathematical model that embodies a set of statistical assumptions concerning the generation of sample data.

4 Facial action coding system (FACS). Based on a system originally developed by a Swedish anatomist named Carl-Herman Hjortsjö. It was later adopted by Paul Ekman and Wallace V. Friesen, and published in 1978: https://www.paulekman.com/facial-action-coding-system/

5 https://en.wikipedia.org/wiki/Photogrammetry

6 https://stretchsense.com

7 Rachel Abramowitz – 'Avatar's Animated Acting', *Los Angeles Times*, published online 18 February 2010. http://articles.latimes.com/2010/feb/18/entertainment/la-et-avatar-actors18-2010feb18

5

Building a character in motion capture

PASCAL LANGDALE

Creating a character is the fundamental common function of all actors and there are a handful of well-known tools and systems developed to help actors do this successfully. motion capture has been described as working in film with the head and in theatre with the body. In this chapter we aim to add to the current standard approaches with techniques that help the actor work in mocap under the common challenge of extreme time pressure and minimal information. We include tools to help when faced with no pre-knowledge of the role, and to physically and believably transform into different creatures or characters. Acting is acting. Motion capture is total acting.

Contributors – America Young (stunts, actor and cinematics director of mocap and voice), Richard Dorton (actor, USA casting director, director, mocap teacher for The Mocap Vaults), Paul-William Mawhinney (actor, performance capture tutor at The Mocap Vaults), Gareth Taylor (actor, games and theatre director, specialist movement teacher for The Mocap Vaults) and Oliver Hollis-Leick (creative director, actor, co-founder of The Mocap Vaults, mocap director at Saber Interactive).

If you've trained in a drama school or taken courses and workshops, the likelihood is that you have been taught in processes that focus primarily on psychological motivation with the belief that the body will naturally follow. It's possible that it goes further to say that physicality beyond your natural range is a threat to truth. If, on the other hand, you have been trained in corporeal acting – mime and clown for example – you may be at the other end of the spectrum, trained to believe that either the language of mime is privileged knowledge or that physical storytelling must be highly expressive.

Motion capture is the most demanding of all forms of acting: You must deliver a performance that is psychologically motivated and physically *embodied*. You must also do this in an empty space, with an absent audience.

America Young can therefore state that it is 'a black box theatre and 360 degrees', where actors have to create a reality in an empty space encumbered by unflattering mocap suits and uncomfortable head-mounted cameras.

> The best thing about it, it's only about performance. How many times have you done the best performance [in film or TV], and it's out of focus … the camera missed it. In mocap it's not missed. Seventy cameras. You don't have to go again for wardrobe and hair. And that's the best gift, there's nothing else but you and the creating of the world.
>
> AMERICA YOUNG

As we discussed in Chapters 2 and 3, 'embodiment' is the physical and psychological inhabitation of another person, character or creature. Your job as an actor is to take the characteristics indicated by any relevant source and use any effective tools that physically change your behaviour accordingly. In this chapter we touch on animals, shapes, music, rhythm and breath, but any approach that proves to work for you must not be excluded. If it works – that's the tool. Experience and a highly trained mind–body connection eventually mean the correct choices are almost automatic and instinctive. Richard Dorton, who is known for playing hundreds of non-human characters, has 'archetypes that I know so well that I can immediately draw from'. Whichever approach you choose, the end goal is embodiment. The rest is largely a question of two types of experience – your experience of observation in daily life and your professional experience as an actor. Both of which will decide how well you perform when you have little to no time to work on a character.

Embodied performances can be applicable to the subtlety of film, but remember motion capture is a physical medium. As we have shown in the animation chapter, stillness is death. This is as true for Mickey Mouse in *The Sorcerer's Apprentice* (Fantasia, 1940) as for the latest video game cinematic of near filmic subtlety. It remains only a question of degree.

Without the physical skills described in the previous chapters, and the techniques to make the use of those skills automatic, improvised and compelling, you will be at sea in the volume.

A mocap actor needs techniques that can be used with a lead time of a few days or a few minutes, with a flexibility that can have you 'turn on a dime' playing multiple characters or creatures if required.

Here follow the basic, interrelated ways of approaching building a character, but as you will see, all are searching ultimately to make the link between psychological and physical truth.

Figure 5.1 *However you choose and apply techniques to create a believable embodied character, the link between physical and psychological must be the final goal. (Photo by Archis Achrekar. Courtesy of Centroid Motion Capture.)*

How to build a physically embodied character

While evidence supports embodiment – that there is no binary split between mind and body – this perspective has yet to gain popular acceptance in mainstream acting training. In this chapter we will keep to more commonly used terms to describe the two broad approaches that actors take to building a character ready for the mocap stage. Keep these summaries in mind as you read on.

Inside-out

Based on the system founded by Stanislavski, this approach means establishing psychological motivation, through script analysis and improvisation. It has become the standard approach to building a character for screen and stage in the Western world. Inside-out approaches use words to describe behaviour. Emotion is considered the natural product of living in the given circumstances pursuing an established goal.

Inside-out relies on a mix of mental analysis, personal experience, research and instinct to guide the actor to try out a variety of behavioural choices.

Outside-in

This approach relies on the body using physicality and externally visible techniques. Outside-in uses physical behaviour, rather than psychological analysis, to discover character.

These systems are often based on the work of schools of mime or movement analysis. Gilles Monteil studied in the systems of both Marcel Marceau and Etienne Decroux – pivotal figures in French mime. Gareth Taylor trained at Lecoq. These systems depend on understanding what the body is communicating, and train actors to have exacting control over physical storytelling. The heritage of Western physical storytelling stretches back to the Greeks but as an approach it can be found in performance styles across cultures. Laban technique must also be included here. Most often associated with dance notation, it is in fact a well-established system of movement analysis highly useful for creating or defining characters through physical qualities of movement. More modern still is the 'Alba technique' developed by Susana Bloch from the early 1990s. The technique of 'Alba Emoting' induces emotion through science-based physical changes, such as specific respiratory, postural and facial behaviours.

The universal challenge: bridging the gap

You can name an action, describe the characteristics and place yourself into the world of the character, but the *how* of the physicality will remain.

You can pick a way of walking, a silhouette, define movement qualities and clear physical storytelling, but the *why* of the psychology will remain.

It is possible to make a list of a character's motivation and characteristics, and from that then try different physical tools to create behaviours that fit. Likewise, physical techniques can suggest psychological explanations that can be assessed for consistency with the character. Either way your job is to bring the two together for physical embodiment suited to motion capture.

This is not a new problem either. One of the biggest conflicts between the first proponents of the Stanislavski Method in America was between Stanislavski's early work, which focused on emotional recall and an 'inside-out' approach, and his later work that focused on physicality. This led to the work of Meisner and Chekhov, which went some way to bridge the gap between the two. Meisner is known for helping free the actor to be present enough so they are truly physically and emotionally in the moment and able to listen. Chekhov made extensive use of imagination and psychophysical gesture, creating a link between the emotional meaning of physicality and the character's behaviour.

As the character already exists, at least in the animator's mind, an actor must always translate what is described to them with words and images into a physical and performable reality. These clues can suggest physicality and appropriate physical exercises that normally lie outside formal method training.

Where to start

What colour are your pants? What's the axe like? Can you describe it? How do you breathe? – that's most important. . . . You'll find the voice. Nothing is wrong. We have to go into imagination . . .

RICHARD DORTON

I always take the psychological approach first and then I'll work it out – I'll let the ripple effect then start to affect my body.

PAUL-WILLIAM MAWHINNEY

First gather as much crucial information as possible. Focus on critical information, not endless backstory!

OLIVER HOLLIS-LEICK

Richard Dorton finds breathing is a key element in defining a character. As rehearsal can be short or non-existent, and the scene can be starting 'in the middle', Richard starts with how the character is going to move, with the physical, with what external elements there are that might affect physicality. That starts with breath.

Gareth Taylor's first step, when he is building a character, is to look at which Laban qualities are dominant in the character. Using the elements of weight, space and time, he decides both the predominant physical behaviour not only as it is shown in gesture, locomotion and attention, but also psychology.

For instance, a powerful presence, who normally slowly turns their head, would be classified as a character showing strong, direct and sustained Laban qualities. They have a solidity to them, a presence of indefatigability (think Marlon Brando in *Apocalypse Now*). What if this hides a super-fast, 'sudden' thought process?

[I]t might be that I want the slow, direct quality, and the heaviness to hide how quickly and lightly the mind is working. So I'm applying motion factors to body, mind, and feeling, to make character decisions. I find a kind of rough state – a starting point.

GARETH TAYLOR

Oliver Hollis-Leick's approach is to research, using whatever time and means are available. This can include material from the animation team or diving into online videos, particularly for physical clues.

The script can be the inspiration for a chosen approach as much as a character breakdown, or the stated Archetype. The character's lines might hold clues as to the qualities of their thought processes. Efficient delivery of technical language, short 'barks' (commands) and smooth persuasion can all be analysed using Laban terms of reference, animal frames of reference, or any other 'outside-in' approach. Oliver points out that language is only the end result, that although they come from a subconscious source, this source can be identified from the external evidence: 'When you are given a text, be a detective. What does your character say about themselves, what do other characters say about themselves, what do they say about your character?' (Oliver Hollis-Leick).

Unlike a purely psychological approach, the following exercises must be physically tested, explored and rehearsed in preparation or in situ, allowing the physical to inform the psychological rather than the other way around. The guiding principle is neatly summarized by Oliver: 'Words bubble up from down below. The thoughts we have in our head ... 99 per cent don't come out as words. Often when we are speaking, we are lying, or at least maintaining our appearance' (Oliver Hollis-Leick).

Linking character to physicality

Once you have the psychological and physical clues drawn from the character outline, images and text, how do you then make the link with your physicality? How do you move from the conceptual stage to the physical stage? Here are four exercises to help align the physical with the psychological and how that comes across to help tell the story.

Establishing a silhouette

I'm always going to consider the silhouette in motion capture. And I always use the Lecoq idea of starting from the floor, and working up. I look at the contact of the feet with the ground and then that will have an impact on where my weight is. That leads into the Laban direction I will favour. Then you have a space to exist in.

GARETH TAYLOR

All mocap actors of any experience will vouch for the value of working on a character's silhouette. This is often the most basic visual reference an animation team will give to you. What pose does the character land in when coming to a stop or a rest? How does that pose communicate the nature of the character to the player? If you are playing the hero in a game with the player in a third-person perspective, remember the player will be spending a lot of time looking at you from behind. Does the silhouette deliver what it needs to from this view? Here we will consider archetypes and shapes further and discuss the centre of balance or 'Laban direction' in the next section.

If you have worked on 'An exercise on silhouettes' in Chapter 2, you will likely have noticed that putting your body into certain shapes makes you think of a variety of archetypes. 'Y' might be a bodybuilder, 'I' may be a military character or a strict teacher, a zig-zag may be a drug addict, or a trickster. As in the earlier chapter, Oliver Hollis-Leick introduces his actors as to *why* we associate certain shapes with certain qualities, as part of his teaching process.

As we have shown, shapes found in nature can trigger a strong approach or avoidance mechanism that is established in the 'old' brain, the amygdala. It is the amygdala that delivers that strong pre-cognitive response to spiders and snakes, even if you are in a country where they pose absolutely no threat or are behind thick glass in a display case. Animators have always known this, and in the early days of film it's clear that actors did too. Think of the shape of Nosferatu's spikey irregular fingers in deep shadow, or the wicked witch of the west. These archetypes, 'dark father' and 'dark mother', are repeated in story after story and often possess physical qualities that are angular and irregular – the zig-zag of the 'Z', manifesting in irregular full-body counter-poised shapes as well as local irregular pointed shapes of fingers or teeth.

Knowing about these deep-seated reactions to basic shapes needn't lead you to arbitrary choices, but rather confirm where your instinct and trial and error are leading you. Then you can make a defendable choice to go with the archetype or against it, rather than a quick assumption.

The character's Laban direction and Lecoq's push and pull

Try this: Stand in your natural pose. Relax and breathe. Set off and walk.

What did you notice?

Walking is controlled falling. An act of faith as you interrupt your fall with each step. You need to have your weight beyond your centre of balance in order to start the whole process. Where was your weight? Try it again, and this time take note of where you have to shift your weight to start walking.

Most students have their weight behind them and so have to shift their weight forward to move. At its most extreme, some people actually take a small step back in order to push themselves forward. Both of these delay the offset of the movement and aren't very heroic. A player isn't going to feel very heroic if their character takes a whole second to get going. A Hero archetype normally has a forward direction pre-disposition. In game, this means that they start moving in the chosen direction the moment that movement is triggered by the character's need, which is triggered by the player's need. We will cover this more technically in Chapter 6, 'Video game locomotion', but it's enough to know for now, that where your centre of weight is placed has a strong effect on your character's movement and correlates with character psychology and motivation.

Laban classified these directions – forward, backward and lateral. Jacques Lecoq believed a fundamental connection of movement existed between everything in a relationship between push and pull. It's what he believed creates drama.

Try the exercise again, and this time imagine there is a rope or bungee tethered to your torso providing a constant tension. Then set off to walk and make notes on what happens physically *and psychologically.*

- Tethered at your back, walk forward feeling the pull back.
- Tethered at your front, walk forward feeling the pull forward.
- Tethered at your back, walk forward pulling against the tether but pushing against a force opposing you.
- Tethered at your front, walk forward being pulled forward but feeling a force also holding you back.
- Tethered at one side more than the other, walk forward
- Tethered at both sides, one stronger than the other.

Once you have done this you will notice how you make links between your physicality and a narrative or psychological mindset. What's behind you is associated with a fixed past and what's ahead, the future in which you have agency. This is as literal as it is psychological. Some describe it like 'home' vs 'unknown'.

Feeling a tether pulling you back whilst pushing forward against a force can make you feel like someone who has a strong tie to their past, but who is driven forward with great purpose.

Reverse the forces, and you feel like someone unwilling to commit. How subtle or broad you make this is up to your choices over character and the style of the production or any knowledge of the size of shot.

The character's animal

Once you've spent a few weeks working on embodying different animal physicalities as outlined in Chapter 2, you can begin to add suitable speech, either improvised or learned, all mediated by the animal physicality.

Consider the character you have been given and work with the text. You may have an instinct that animal work will be your way 'in'. Let the physical character mediated by your animal physicality drive the text, not the other way around. That's the only way your work will have an effect. If you just do the text adding just a hint of your physicality, then the work will have been for nothing. We're *experimenting* here so you need to be playful and free, not end-gaining.

Eventually, you will read a piece of text or find a character and then you will start to ask, 'Which animal would this character be?' Then you can go and find that animal and repeat all this work with the specific aim of embodying the existing character you have been given.

The more animals you study, the more reference material you will have in your head. On a mocap set, you often have very little time to get to know your character. The more animals you know, the better.

Psychophysical

As the work of Michael Chekhov suggests, there is another angle from which you can analyse, categorize and embody psychologically driven physical behaviour. In short, working in the area where psychology and physical behaviour meet. Embodying physicalities far from your habitual self seems dangerous and the route to fakery and failure. It's easy to become quite trapped in a safe 'neutral' physicality, something often demanded as part of theatre and film training. However, mocap acting requires a boldness and willingness to try the assumed impossible. Fifty years of behavioural psychology and neurology should be therefore considered a treasure trove for a transformational actor. This would have been approved by Stanislavski, who famously noted, 'Art should be on good terms with science.' Here is an exercise that keys in to a very different way of working.

Approach/avoid character exercise

This exercise is a development of a study that examined approach-avoidance motivation.[1] Make a list of all the salient concepts, characters and relationships in your character's world drawn from the character breakdown and the script and free imagination. This should include universal concepts not explicitly in the narrative, such as love, God, family members and so on. If you don't have someone to read the list back to you then pre-record the list, allowing three or four seconds between each word.

Making sure you have space around you, stand with your eyes closed.

As yourself, listen to the list and if a word is one that attracts you, take one step forward and back to your start position. If it is a word that repels you, step back and then return to your start position. You may already be thinking where these reactions may differ from the perspective of the character. Good.

You have now identified relationships that give you a psychophysical approach or avoidance reaction. If done without overthinking it, these reactions are coming from the 'old' brain, the limbic system which is concerned with constantly evaluating whether something is a benefit, a threat or of no concern. This occurs pre-cognitively as the limbic system is the thing that makes us able to jump out of the way of a cyclist or a tiger without consciously deciding first.

Now repeat the exercise from the perspective of *the character* and note where the choice to move forward or back *differs from your own instinct*. Question whether that fits in with what you know about the character or if it reveals something you didn't know. For instance, *your* reaction to 'home' might be to step forward. Without thinking too hard, you knew from the perspective of the character that you should step back. Then, you may ask yourself 'Why?'

Establishing these relationships can be the start of mediating your behaviour around another character or environment that is associated directly or indirectly with one of these words. For example, you may decide that your character's new platoon commander would be associated with 'amateur', an implicit subject in the character's world concerning other things. Perhaps your character stepped forward on 'amateur', and you reasoned that was because your character knew they could take advantage of naive incompetents in any situation. If it was *you* in the platoon, being led by someone you didn't trust would worry you. In *your* world, you would step back. Knowing this can affect how your character behaves towards their commander, even though it is not explicit in the script.

This doesn't mean that you must step forward or back during a scene or even deliberately show something. It is rather that the urge, the instinctive reaction, is felt and its origins understood, whether as character examination in preparation, during rehearsal or the take. Or all three.

You discovered it using your own approach-avoid reaction to bring an aspect of the character's values into relief by comparison.

Bringing the character to the mocap stage

Whether you have had a chance to work on your character at home, in rehearsal or are confronted with the need for an instant characterization handed to you at the end of a long day, the character needs to be there the moment before action is called. There are a few media-specific elements that interrupt what might be a smooth entry into a film, TV or stage scene.

Each capture sequence starts and ends with a 'T-pose' (see Chapter 1).

Figure 5.2 *Each capture sequence starts and ends with a 'T-pose'. (Photo by Archis Achrekar. Courtesy of Centroid Motion Capture.)*

All props are laid at a distance from the performer. When any combination of capture, sound and reference camera is called as rolling, the performer collects any props and moves to 'first position'. As every second can cost more than the costs of a similar blockbuster movie second, you must be ready and embody the character as quickly as possible. Then the director can call action and, importantly, the animators responsible for cleaning, solving and retargeting have a clear starting point. Often animators are instructed to process everything between T-poses. If you are still chatting to another actor, or need extra time to get into character, this is someone else's time and production money you are wasting. As the mocap data can cost from \$10 to \$35 per second (at time of writing) every second literally counts.

As a result, mocap performers often find keys or triggers that can get them into an embodied state quickly, or even make do as an instant characterization element if required. Laban, archetypes and animal studies can work depending on your experience, amount of rehearsal and practice. More universal, perhaps, is the use of Breath, Rhythm and Music to stimulate a physically present performance in short order.

Breath

At the most fundamental we use breath to signify that the digital model is alive and gives that illusion of life for digital image. On a deeper level it's my go-to for the start of every single take – I'll check in with my breath because my breath is linked to my emotional state, my mental state, and my physical state. I look at it like a hot-wire start to those other engines. So if I want to get myself into an emotional state I will find a breathing pattern that will emulate that emotional state and breathe like that.

PAUL-WILLIAM MAWHINNEY

[B]reath is your gateway. I think breath is the thing that makes whatever the mind thinks, or whatever the body feels, a lived experience. It connects them.

GARETH TAYLOR

Once you work out how a character breathes, then you are a lot of the way there.

RICHARD DORTON

Breath can be the easiest thing to overlook. However, as every teacher here states, it's a fundamental aspect of grounding or dropping into character and context however subtle or extreme. Running into a scene at a squat, avoiding enemy fire needs your breath to be that of someone who has been running and moving energetically under a state of threat. It is unlikely that your starting point is deep meditative breathing. Or even just your regular unattended breathing.

Rhythm

Rhythm is another useful preparation. You have a natural rhythm of doing things that changes through the day. How you put dishes away can change according to how caffeinated you are, and rhythm can have a similar effect. Finger clicking, foot tapping or mentally marking a rhythm in the moments before and after the initial T-pose can change your breathing placement and pace. Learn odd count rhythms if you are unfamiliar with anything other than the ubiquitous four count and three counts of all Western rock, classical and pop music. Listen to Dave Brubeck's 'Take Five' album where he explores five- and seven-count rhythms. Raga can have patterns in cycles of five, seven, nine or ten beats. There's a flamenco twelve-count rhythm that allegedly counts out the interplay between the fast heartbeat of an unborn child and the slower heartbeat of their mother. This is an irregular halting rhythm, and as such can create a sense of unease created by more variation of tempo. In contrast, regular rhythms have a predictability to them that can lend a smooth quality to your behaviour at different speeds. Try performing a mundane task, counting out and timing your movements to match a five-count rhythm compared with a four-count rhythm and you will instantly see and feel the difference. Remember to note how it changes you physically *and* what it makes you *feel*.

Music

> I asked them to play 'Stayin' Alive' for a particular character when doing a walk cycle. Music has an amazing effect on people. It's a great tool. . . . It has reality distorting properties. It is so powerful.
>
> OLIVER HOLLIS-LEICK

> Music is crucial. I have a heroic walk, what do I use? The *Avengers* theme tune. I can tap into my playlist. I use it in my classes for animal work. What makes you cry, what makes you scared? I use dance a lot too, as I have a dance background. . . . We all love music.
>
> RICHARD DORTON

As Richard notes, music is so pervasive that we can recall the rhythm, melody and 'feel' or 'vibe' of music we know well.

If you've ever walked somewhere listening to music you will notice your stride will often drift to match the music style, if not rhythm. Go back to the mundane task of the rhythm exercise and listen to music that you know affects you. Watch how it changes your emotional mood and physical behaviour. Pick another piece of music to observe the differences. Having a 'playlist' in your mind, as Richard describes it, can be a fantastic tool to use before a scene to give that physical energy you need to instantly run on all cylinders.

A total performance is always useful

Most four-legged creatures have radically different bone proportions from those of a human. Our closest animal relatives have proportionally shorter legs to body and much longer arms, which is why mocap actors wear arm extensions when playing apes and monkeys. Sometimes your creature can talk. Here is the border between what an actor can usefully offer in mocap and what they can offer in performance. Applying an equal thoroughness to creatures will ensure you are offering not just physical data, which may or may not be easily transferable, but you are also offering the character of the creature. An animator may gain inspiration from your voice, the reference video of your body and facial performance.

Figure 5.3 *Limb extensions can be used to play creatures with different body shapes, for example quadrupeds. (Actor Ace Ruele. Courtesy of Creature Bionics. Photo by Archis Achrekar. Courtesy of Centroid Motion Capture.)*

Summary

Whatever approach or acting techniques you use to build a character, at some point your physicality will need to match their physical heritage, shape and movement of the character, to a scale and level of truth that matches the story and size of shot. This is no different from the ideals of theatre acting, with this one exception. All that mocap sees is the movement of markers in space to indicate the movement of the skeleton in space. Therefore, physicality is the primary form of communication in the motion capture volume.

In such a collaborative process you are often the outsider coming in at the later stages and need the tools, confidence and freedom to deliver with little preparation or rehearsal. Respect the sheer talent of the people who brought this character to you, but also respect your right to be counted among them. Know that you have a right to create something more complete, if slightly different, from what they have yet imagined. What's true in one job may not be true in another. So. Ask questions. Ask questions. Ask questions.

> I will ask as many questions as I need to ask, to make sure I'm giving the right delivery of performance ... what I tell students is that this doesn't come across as an insecure actor not knowing all the answers, it comes across as a professional who knows what they need to find out ... in order to be able to deliver the best version of the character you can.
>
> GARETH TAYLOR

> I will always ask for what I need, a squeaky wheel and all that. Worst case scenario is, 'I'm sorry we have no time left, move on', in which case that's all you can do.
>
> PAUL-WILLIAM MAWHINNEY

All the approaches in this chapter demand study in their own right and are used here as examples for further exploration and training. Having these basic tools available in the midst of a highly collaborative and often constraining media is the key to successful motion capture acting.

However, the exercises and the character tools described in this book are not exclusive of any other approach that achieves the same results. I know of one actor who changed their behaviour when the director asked them to change what kind of fruit they were – from melon to orange, I recall. *Any* process or exercise that makes the link between physicality and psychology embodying the reality of the character in the scene is useful. If it works, it works.

Chapter 5 takeaways

Embody	Don't get restricted to either 'outside-in' or 'inside-out'. Use whatever techniques that work to have a physically, emotionally and psychologically integrated character. If it works, it works.
Explore	Learn and practise Laban, Lecoq's pull/push, silhouettes, animal studies, approach/avoid.
Quick access tools	Never forget it in your checklist and use these as a key to hit the ground running: breath, rhythm and music.
Always act	Even if you know your capture data is unlikely to be useful (creature work for example), still deliver your best performance possible from initial to end 'T-pose'. You are a primary team member who shares creative responsibility with the animator. Ask questions to get the answers you need.

Note

1   'Individual Differences in Approach and Avoidance Movements: How the Avoidance Motive Influences Response Force'; Puca, Rosa Maria; Rinkenauer, Gerhard; Breidenstein, Christian. *Journal of Personality* 74:4 August 2006.

6

Video game locomotion

PASCAL LANGDALE

Video games require the player to be in control. Any moves the player makes – such as walks, turns, runs and strafes (running in a crouch or near squat) must occur without a moment's delay. This requires the creation of a library of thousands of repeated moves that can be drawn on for an exhaustive range of movements. Moreover, every move must be symmetrical, able to be blended with gameplay animation at any moment and remain in character. These 'locomotions' are a highly technical aspect of motion capture work, often drawn out over many days, requiring immense fitness and physical control. This chapter helps the actor understand the demands and the efficient ways to deliver a consistent character that never disappoints.

Contributors – Marc Morisseau (motion editor at Lightstorm Entertainment) and Richard Dorton (actor, USA casting director, director, mocap teacher for The Mocap Vaults).

Locomotions – the consequence of interactivity

The principal difference between a video game and a film is interactivity. Interactivity is the key driver behind the culture, priorities and practical undertaking of game making. How a player's character performs even the most basic of movements from walking to opening a door makes up the greatest proportion of most game play experiences. Unlike cinematics, which we tackle in the next chapter, these are actions that occur 'in-game' and are triggered by choices the player makes while moving their character through the game world. Locomotions are a consequence of interactivity. They deserve both our attention and respect, as one of the most challenging aspects of a performer's role in game creation.

Why is it challenging? Marc Morisseau points out in film you can spend time and money refining and perfecting a single shot, frame by frame, anchored in the real world. In contrast, a player can move their character in any direction and look in any direction in a completely invented three-dimensional digital world. Marc describes it like building bridges from one moment to another: 'Where a character stops has to be exactly where they start up again,' down to the very footprint. '[L]ike building bridges over a canyon that is changing in shape and size as you are building.'

Locomotions themselves might seem simple. Walking, jogging, running, for example. The need for the player to be able to move in any direction at any time with an increase or decrease in speed means the game engine will have to blend the motions between multiple locomotions. These include physical actions such as turning on the spot, turning and walking in all directions, turning and running in all directions, and coming to a stop. Each may need to be performed holding a different weapon. Now include combat moves or repeated actions such as riding a horse, driving a car, or even opening a door – possibly each with multiple variables of weapon or physical condition and we are quickly numbering thousands of moves.

Don't think it's just a question of banging them out. Much of the player's experience of the character is based on these movements, and so the characterization must be present and consistent through all locomotions. The character is unlikely to tire, and must be at 100 per cent reactivity and energy, consistent through all locomotions. If the character does tire, then that too will generate a list of tired locomotions. How the move is performed, its quality and form, also have to be characterful enough but generic enough to work in any context. Every one of them must be technically correct, starting and ending in a specific foot and body placement.

As a result, locomotion shoots can occur a few times each month over the course of a couple of years or more, as the game's demands change,

Figure 6.1 *Locomotions like strafing must be repeated with each weapon the character has as an option. (Photo by Archis Achrekar. Courtesy of Centroid Motion Capture.)*

or new lead animators change direction. It is one of the most captured and repetitive (and/or demanding) of all motion capture jobs.

If you're lucky, you have another performer, but often it's just you. You can expect a team of two actors to get through 150 to 175 locomotions in a day – the higher number assuming it's the simpler stuff.

What skills do you need to deliver good locomotions?

Like other aspects of motion capture, the actor needs a good sense of their body in space, and to be able to hit physical positions accurately all day. It's likely you are doing all the moves for a character performed by another, perhaps well-known, actor who performs in the cinematic sequences. Therefore the task is to take the essence of the source actor and make it a practical physicality that not only provides a clear standing pose, but that can also affect the performance in thousands of moves.

Stamina is vital, as you can probably now understand. Marc says that lead actors rarely perform their own locos, not just because of time and schedule, but also because the level of stamina needed is something that is not in their skillset.

> Cinematic actors who've done in-game realise how challenging it is. Five years of working in-game is like twenty years on your body! Once you've done a day of sprints, crouches and Crouch runs etc. you'll know what I'm talking about! Younger performers are often used.
>
> RICHARD DORTON

Most games involve conflict resolved in hand-to-hand combat, with blades and/or guns. Being trained in martial arts, swordsmanship, staff, and all the variations of gun handling and military moves of different cultures and even historic periods, can mean that you will be

Figure 6.2 *A day of sprints, crouches, crouch runs (strafes), crawls and jumps is physically extremely demanding. (Photo by Archis Achrekar. Courtesy of Centroid Motion Capture.)*

seen as the Swiss army knife of locomotions. It will give you an edge landing that first role and if you deliver, you will be asked back time and time again.

How to do the job

It is unlikely that you will know what locomotions are planned until the morning of the shoot. This is your first opportunity to ask questions and make requests that will help you deliver the range and quality of locomotions the animator or director wants.

First of all, you need to know the character you are playing. You will be able to see what the character looks like, so you can work out the range of movement possible. If they have huge sharp-edged shoulder armour, for example, reaching up might push the armour into their face, so now is the time to discuss alternatives. Bending from the sides instead, for example. Whatever the solution to physical constraints, these choices can become part of the characterization. If the role has been played in the cinematics by another actor, it is now routine that you can access video reference material of the actor walking and running, at least. From this you must establish a style that you can repeat consistently across a range of physical moves that matches the actor's physicality close enough. This is a standard aspect of a stunt person's skillset. A quick rehearsal with the director will help to establish quite how much unique characterization is acceptable. Let the developer adjust the performance. Put the personality into the loco and let them choose if they want it or by how much. Marc Morisseau points out that this early stage is a chance to establish a common language with someone who may have a very different background from you. On *Call of Duty*, Marc remembers establishing a difference between 'faster' and 'peppy'. Use whatever works that can adjust your performance throughout the day.

You can also request to change the order of the shoot. Most teams don't care when the locomotions are shot, only that they are captured that day and are of good quality. Some actors choose to start the day with the hard physical moves, some end the day with them; some prefer to put them before lunch break. Get to know what works best for you, compromise with any co-actor and ask. According to Marc, surprisingly few actors do this, many just throw themselves at it. The most experienced arrange the day to work for them, however.

Two deceptively simple locomotion exercises

These exercises are intended to illustrate how even something simple, like the player wanting to turn the character and walk in a new direction, demands well-executed generic locomotions. These must obey both animation constraints (starting and stopping in the same position and shape) and immediacy.

Preparation: Tape out an even cross about 2 foot by 2 foot, using masking or painter's tape. If you're outside, a chalk cross will work, as long as the lines are straight and at right angles. It can be helpful to have a cue to perform the exercise, so either get a partner to clap, or record yourself, waiting ten seconds or so between a series of single claps (so you can repeat the exercise without resetting the recording).

Turning on the spot

Exercise: Stand in the neutral hero stance you found in the silhouette exercise (Chapter 2). Make sure the centre of your body is directly above the centre of the cross. When you hear a clap, turn 90 degrees and face the side. Now look down. See how far you have moved from the centre of the cross. The animator will expect you to hit the same body shape directly above the centre of the cross, otherwise they will need to correct it later. Repeat at 180 degrees and even 270 degrees. Now make it look natural and hit your hero pose without tension.

Moving off (and turn and walk)

Preparation: Stand in your hero pose. When you hear a clap, you have to walk forward. Then return to your cross. Note if you had to transfer any weight before moving forward. Was there a delay between the clap and the move? Do it again and try to place your weight so you can move without any re-adjustment. Repeat with the next clap. Once you have mastered this, repeat but turning to walk off at a 90 degree and then a 180 degree from your start position.

Using real-time and reference video

Real-time is used extensively for locomotions by both actors and the animation team, as it's very useful to see how movements show up on the rig. As mentioned above, seeing your character's shoulder spikes puncture their head is a much more effective way of learning the physical constraints and how you should move. If you don't have real-time and virtual cameras, Marc says you 'can guarantee you'll be going back for re-shoots'. He recommends using real-time to establish limits to physicality but lean into the video recording for the best reference of your performance.

Although locomotions are repeated and largely generic moves, you won't be replaced by AI or procedural animation any time soon. Procedural animation and AI still can't make a character. It can tell a system to spin a revolver, but it can't bring the character to life. Marc recommends that actors should focus on what makes the character unique. You have a lifetime of references and experience that machine learning still can't compete with.

Finally, one last piece of advice from Marc Morrisseau:

Know your character and the game style before you turn up. Put more work into preparing the part, not playing the part.

Chapter 6 takeaways

The player is controller and audience	'Locomotions' – all the routine movements from walking to gun handling – need to be captured and animated. This normally makes up the majority of any game experience.
Locomotions are technical	You need great physical awareness and control to match positions and create symmetrical movements, working within character restraints and shapes.
Locomotions need some character	The animation director will help decide how much character. However, your character choices need to be applicable in as wide a range of circumstances as possible and always filled with the energy of goal-oriented intention.
It's a workout of repetition	You can perform hundreds of moves in a day, some can require remarkable endurance. Change the order of shot list to deliver the best results. Negotiate with other actors for the best compromise.

7

Cinematics

John Dower

Cinematics are the storytelling and character development elements of video games. As the name suggests, they are often highly visually arresting dramatic scenes, akin to what we might expect from film, television, or stage. However, whether stand-alone, or interactive, they present specific acting challenges. Creating compelling and believable character work in an alienating mocap studio requires huge inspiration, imaginary leaps and 100 per cent commitment. In this chapter, leading directors will discuss how they work in the volume and what their expectations are from their actors. We will then expand on the different modes – motion capture, performance capture, acting to pre-recorded audio and facial capture. The reader will come to understand how even when working with virtual cameras, stand-in props and stripped-down sets, performers can create memorable performances in cinematic scenes.

Contributors – America Young (stunts, actor and cinematics director of mocap and voice), Steve Kniebihly (cinematics director), Kate Saxon (theatre, television and cinematics director), Yuji Shimomura (action and cinematics director), David Footman (cinematics director at Ubisoft) and Hideaki Itsuno (game director at Capcom).

Directing in motion capture is different from other performance media

When I first started working in games as a cinematics director, I had come from the world of film, television and, previously, theatre. I knew little about games. I soon learnt that storytelling in those media is *linear* and that video games was conversely an *interactive* medium. I had to get my head around the fact that, as director, I was not the pre-eminent storyteller in the room. The *player* was. It took a while to get used to. Not only that, but the position as director in mocap was much more collaborative and other heads of department were as or more important.

Usually, the game designers have been developing the game for a while before the director is brought in and the animator is usually the senior person too.

> Film directors probably have a more difficult time with the transition as they are used to being in control. In TV, the director is a little like a substitute teacher, so collaboration is more natural. Animators and game designers might have been working with the idea for a couple of years, so you can be the enthusiasm they've forgotten and bring in fresh ideas.
>
> AMERICA YOUNG

Directing in games therefore does not suit all directors, as they have to get used to not always being top dog. I find it a freeing position and enjoy working with animators, writers, creative directors and games designers. As we've discussed in the previous chapters, the animator is the one responsible for taking the performances on to the screen and the games designers are the ones to ultimately control how the finished game functions for the player. However, as you'll see, there is also a new breed of directors coming up with different expectations.

Animators and games designers are used to being in control and don't always want directors coming in and having too much influence. Because of this, and what they might see as an unnecessary expense, sometimes they won't use a mocap performance director at all. We'll outline the challenges for the actor when that happens in the next chapter.

However, having outlined how different the role of the director can be in cinematics, let's start with some definitions.

What are cinematics?

Sometimes also called a cutscene, cinematics are the storytelling elements of games. They are often stand-alone scenes which develop the characters, move the story along, have an expositional function, or simply explain to the player what the next mission is to be. However, they are usually far from mundane. 'Games cinematics are rarely kitchen sink realism: they're more often epic and stakes are high, so playing clear motivation on the line and in the moment is key. Shakespeare's characters are often good touchstones for many game characters' (Kate Saxon).

Director Steve Kniebihly sees the role of the director becoming more important in video games:

If you're working on a game like 'Resident Evil', it's a franchise . . . you as the director are the keeper of the narrative . . . all you can do is voice your concerns in the face of game director changes. You need to know how a game is made, how the gameplay works, because that will affect your cinematic. There's some specific gameplay constraints. Fifteen years ago the overall director of the game was the game director, but now the cinematic director/performance director has more of a role and more responsibility.

Sometimes cinematic scenes are interactive, having moments the player can control, cameras they can adjust or offering them choices. An example of this is *quicktime events*. These are where the player performs actions on the control device shortly after the appearance of an on-screen instruction/prompt. It allows for limited control of the game character during cinematic sequences. As an example, some games made by Supermassive use these in their cinematics (e.g. *Until Dawn*).

Another way that cinematics can be interactive is due to the power of game or real-time engines, mentioned in the animation chapter. Previously, cinematics were like pre-recorded videos and the game engine had to switch from interactive mode to play them like a film. As David Footman (cinematics director at Ubisoft) says:

> Video games have changed a lot in the last decade. We used to use fully rendered cinematics, which played like a video file in the game engine, but now we are in 'run-time'. There are three levels of these – 1) High-level run-time cinematic which is rendered on the fly. It can have personalised costumes, weapons, scars etc. 2) Animation stations, with gesture systems and lip animations playing through wave-form. 3) Crowd level – more systematic, more AI driven. Mixed characters, some driven by AI, some by a behaviour tree.

So, many games play their cinematic scenes in-engine and the player's interaction continues. Footman adds: 'Run-time allows what the player does to impact the scene. Players are enchanted by, and are coming to expect, causality. How we bring causality into cinematics and facial animation reinforces the 'I am' and the 'I do' into gaming.'

You can see that the player's imprint on the game is highly valued and is becoming expected, even during some cinematics. Regarding the player's interaction, there is something else to remember – you are often playing either the player's avatar or a significant character in their world.

> Here is a key thing to remember about acting in games – you are with the gamers for weeks. The bond is amazing. You become a part of their life. If you are the player's avatar – you help them escape from their world. They are with you in a different way than a film – it's a different and stronger relationship. Remember – in a recession the two things that don't go down in sales are video games and alcohol!!!
>
> AMERICA YOUNG

We don't want to put extra pressure on, but you can see that the responsibility on the actor and animator is considerable. As Young adds: 'As a storyteller that's the gift and the honour you have, to take them on a journey – a life they wouldn't live – is great. However, conversely it means if they don't like your performance they really let you know.'

How are cinematics created?

Let's delve deeper into how a successful cinematic performance is created. Cinematics vary, so let's look at the preparation that goes into them before the shoot.

Figure 7.1 '*Here is a key thing to remember about acting in games – you are with the gamers for weeks. The bond is amazing. You become a part of their life. If you are the player's avatar – you help them escape from their world*' *(America Young). (Photo by Archis Achrekar. Courtesy of Centroid Motion Capture.)*

Some are planned in detail pre-shoot so that the actor is required to deliver to a preconceived brief. A game director like Hideaki Itsuno, who has masterminded the *Devil May Cry* series of games from the second to the fifth instalment, creates a detailed live action storyboard known as pre-visualization or 'previs', expecting the actor to recreate it in the volume. As he says: 'If the quality of the performers' ideas are on par with the ideas of the cinematics director and myself, that's when the actor has more input.' Itsuno's games are full of action and stunts, so it's not surprising that he has found the most efficient way to create his games is to plan in detail ahead. Action and cinematics director Yuji Shimomura similarly prepares meticulously in advance: 'I create live action previs ... I am then able to share my vision with the client. It determines the length and cuts down costs and it means that what clients want and what I am aiming for are the same. In effect I would shoot a movie over 90 minutes long before going into directing the mocap.'

Other games designers may be less prescriptive, particularly in character-led, dialogue-based scenes, only creating previs for their action sequences.

> Performance capture also shares many aspects of theatre in terms of the work space: as a mocap volume is necessarily bare of set, it can feel like an early days rehearsal room for a really cheap production! The joy of this is that it's a space for play and imagination and an actor can give their final performance in that freeing environment.
>
> KATE SAXON

Some directors become embedded in the workflow of the game developer and work for years on a game, as I have been in the past, or are brought in on a freelance basis.

> [Directing cinematics] depends on the gig, studio, working within the dev team or as a freelancer. It means taking care of all the narrative beats in the game. I'm involved in the writing, storyboarding, auditions, technical prep, then on the day directing the shoot like on a movie or TV set. Sometimes I'm involved in the camera animation, sometimes lighting and VFX.
>
> STEVE KNIEBIHLY

The key is to understand how the cinematic scene fits into the game and what its purpose is.

> The collaboration between performance director and lead animator is key: effectively, they are the DOP and designer rolled into one. They may have created animatics, or storyboards that

Figure 7.2 *'The joy is that it's a space for play and imagination and an actor can give their final performance in that freeing environment' (Kate Saxon). (Photo by Archis Achrekar. Courtesy of Centroid Motion Capture.)*

show their ideas, and they will also share the environment art with me and the cast. I find from there, I have freedom to develop ideas with the actors. As long as I stage the scene within the environment that's designed and understand where the characters have come from and are going to in gameplay, staging of the cinematic itself has a lot of freedom.

KATE SAXON

Whether you are working with a director with the freedom that Kate Saxon describes, or you are working to the tighter requirements of previs which you are expected to serve, your job as the performer is to understand what the director and the team are looking for and hopefully to add value to make that performance even better than expected.

A note on preparation

Two things you must remember about video games are – first, they are super secretive for commercial reasons, and second, being an animated medium, the actor is not seen as being the centre of the process. This means that often what the actor needs to help create a great performance in the volume is under-appreciated. As mentioned in the previous chapters, sometimes prep time is very different from what you would expect from working on stage or screen.

> Most of the budget goes to the gameplay. It's still pretty difficult to get a producer to agree to proper rehearsals, even a script reading before the shoot, so you can tweak the lines with the actors. Even casting or testing the chemistry for an ensemble cast. Often the actor will only learn about the character the day before or the hour before, or even when they walk on set – so being adaptable needs to be an actor's skill. It also puts pressure on the director to get the actor to find the character quickly.
>
> STEVE KNIEBIHLY

The secrecy means that anyone who is involved in a game will be asked to sign an NDA: a non-disclosure agreement. These can vary in strength. I've signed NDAs that mean I can't say *anything* about the game I'm working on to *anyone*. When I directed the cutscenes for *007 Legends* for EON/Activision, we were working on scenes inspired by the imminent Bond film *Skyfall* and the scenes connected to that film were so secret that the full script appeared in the hands of a minion of the lawyers, who took the script from a briefcase, showed it to the actors on set, allowed them time to memorize it and then put it back in the briefcase and left! The secrecy and concern for leaks means that NDAs are serious. On the same game we had an actor who was cast one day, tweeted about it that night and was sacked the next day – before even starting work. Don't mess with NDAs!

How does it impact prep? It means developers are very careful about who they send information and scripts to. Every element of the process has to be secure and this can mean that you won't get a script until you arrive on the day of the shoot. Though developers are beginning to better appreciate what actors need to create a good performance, this is a relatively new thing. Although rehearsals and pre-shoot prep does happen more nowadays, it is still the norm that you will get a script in your hands on the day of the shoot. And it might not look like a film or theatre script either. It might be in the form of a previs video or even an Excel spreadsheet with each line in a different box. This is because a line of dialogue is given a file name for the game engine.

David Footman is a new breed of director in mocap, who really appreciates what actors need and has been successful in fighting for it: 'P-cap studios are hostile environments for actors – there is nothing there they need to perform well with. The amount of prep time is huge. Rehearsal time is way more than episodic TV. I have to at least speak to actors in advance.' David is working on big game franchises, so don't be surprised if his expectations do not match your experiences!

So, what does this all mean? It means that the mocap actor must think fast, be flexible and spontaneous. Decisions must be made fast and committed to.

> I look for the trait of flexibility from actors – 'Sure, I'm a peacock, let's do it!' I have found that actors used to a particular theatre approach e.g. Shakespeare have found that more of a challenge since they have a more fixed idea of how their character would play a line.

> AMERICA YOUNG

As you'll have seen in the previous chapters on creating characters, all experienced mocap actors have a range of methods of finding a character and learning lines fast and being open and flexible to change. It's not to say that you won't have time to rehearse, it's just that it will be super concentrated, short, and you'll be expected to be ready to shoot much quicker than you might be used to. All the actors we have interviewed accentuate the positive sides to this and absolutely make the best of it. There is no room for regret, lengthy experimentation or character dissection. It's about quick decision making, a willingness to improvise and to vibe off your fellow actors.

If we are talking about 'generalists', who can play many characters, then they need to be able to be quick to pick up direction and move in an authentic way. Experienced voice actors have similar qualities – they can pick up a script and just sound right. Generalists

Figure 7.3 *There is no room for regret, lengthy experimentation or character dissection. It's about quick decision making, a willingness to improvise and to vibe off your fellow actors. (Photo by Archis Achrekar. Courtesy of Centroid Motion Capture.)*

need to pick up quickly, be in control of their body and be able to communicate with gestures. I have more success with actors from theatre [...] Don't be afraid to ask for what you need to succeed. Be greedy – if you need a prop, a line reading – ask for it. It's crucial to prepare and explore.

DAVID FOOTMAN

This is an echo from Paul-William Mawhinney, Gareth Taylor and Oliver Hollis-Leick from an earlier chapter, who all had the same advice to ask for what they needed in order to be as ready as possible in the time they had to prepare.

The practical differences between mocap, performance capture, facial capture and working with pre-recorded audio

Mocap (body only)

It may be that the animators are intending to apply the facial capture later. Sometimes the voice will be recorded at a different time. Voice actors are used to prioritizing vocal characterization over physical characterization, which means they may well be more at home in the recording studio or booth. Or the voice actor is a star, and sweating away in the volume is not their idea of fun. It must be noted that voice is valued more highly than body in video games and voice actors are usually paid substantially more for their time.

The voice actors actually own it. Do the 'cons' (conventions i.e. Comic-Con), 'get the profile, get more money. ... Voice actors put a lot into it, but if you've done the body performance in in-game and cinematics then it should be shared. For example, in a recent game there was one voice for a character and around seven different people doing various stunts and body performances. However several major game developers will not acknowledge that mocap *is* performance, so don't feel the need for SAG contracts. Several major titles therefore use Union for voice and non-union for body. This is the case in the USA.

AMERICA YOUNG

Don't let that put you off. We believe that the time is coming when physical performance becomes more highly valued. It wasn't long ago that stage and screen actors were strangers to the volume. A lot has changed in the last ten years and the respect for actors in mocap is increasing all the time. Young and Footman are enthusiastic about mocap:

> If it's just mocap/body, I think it's easier to relax, you're not remembering lines or the accent you're performing in. There is a more streamlined approach. You learn the nuance, like a dance. It makes it a more playful vibe because there's less to remember. You can really dig into the physical creativity, focus on finding new ways of storytelling with your body and it's pure fun.

AMERICA YOUNG

> When I have the chance to do scenes 'body-only' it is a joy – actors love it too.

DAVID FOOTMAN

As we mentioned in the animation chapter, there is also a need for actors to populate the rest of the characters in the games – the NPCs (non-player characters), background characters, crowds etc. Remember what animator Ralph Palmer said about these? There is no sub-text. You just play at being your character, making them physically believable.

I think nowadays we are more about casting good actors. That said, if you are being cast as an NPC, you better be good at improvisation and having multiple ways of doing something. You may get cast as a passerby in a game and you may need to do the same action in ten different ways and be ten different characters.

STEVE KNIEBIHLY

Performance capture aka P-cap

You will remember us mentioning that mocap data is charged by the second. It ain't cheap. Now imagine what is required when you have body, face *and* voice being recorded at the same time. The amount of data is increased, the sound department requires a special sound stage, and the quantity of technicians making all of the tech happy is multiplied. 'With Perfcap you will have seven people giving you notes (e.g. cinematics director, sound tech, facial capture animator, voice director etc.). So many different things that you are doing at once – which is harder' (America Young).

But it's not just that. Now what your face is doing is important – not just your body. Added to that, your voice must be the best it can be. Voice in animation – a medium as we've established which relies on creating a sense that the character is alive – is highly scrutinized because the face and body might not communicate everything as believably as live action. The pressure is huge. It's rare that an actor is really strong at all the qualities required.

Steve Kniebihly works on some of the biggest games, so unsurprisingly he deals with bigger budgets and higher expectations than some. However, he seems to be predicting a future where P-cap is far more common.

In my experience the industry is moving towards full perf-cap. We are trying to tell better stories and there is no better way to do that than with full performance capture. You never get the same results if you get the face afterwards. However, there is stuff you can't do with a headcam on, like physical action, stunts – sometimes we do that simultaneously – stunt and actor, with body markers hidden so we can get the reactions. The actor sits in the volume with their body markers covered and trying to react to what the stunt performer is doing. Trying to do that six months later in an ADR booth is much more difficult!

STEVE KNIEBIHLY

The possibility of two people performing elements of the same character simultaneously is a great collaborative challenge and, for many, signals the variety of ways of working in this medium. For Kate Saxon, whether performance capture or motion capture, the skills required are the same:

Most games performances need to be pitched as though to reach a small theatre, not a TV camera lens. One place that we can't put tracking dots onto is an actor's eyeballs, so reactions, feelings and thoughts need to be communicated in expression, both facially and physically. A performance is necessarily an exercise in embodying a character wholly, whether or not the data is being used for only one aspect of it in the final product.

Facial capture

We've talked about facial capture before, but let's just return to it in terms of how it affects the actor working on the floor. Head-mounted cameras are the latest in a line of inventions created for animators who aim to make great facial animation. They haven't been made for the actor's benefit! 'Let me talk about facial. I have a pet peeve – I find HMCs extremely frustrating. They are distracting for performers. When House of Moves (a well-known mocap studio in LA) had a high-density studio with 250 cameras, where actors used facial markers, it was better' (David Footman).

HMCs are often uncomfortable, with a camera – sometimes multiple cameras – and lights, mounted on support bars that stick out in front of your face. You may get used to them, but they hamper movement, especially if there is combat or close contact required. They can render a scene between two lovers into a dance of stag-beetles. If they are knocked out of line, the actor may be asked to go through the indignity of wearing a thick elastic chinstrap to keep them more firmly planted on their head.

So, if you are brought in to do facial capture only – either using your voice, or performing to someone else's – this is stitched together afterwards to make a complete character performance. As mentioned before in the animation chapter, this is sometimes called the

Figure 7.4 *HMCs. You may get used to them, but they hamper movement, especially if there is combat or close contact required. A scene between two lovers can be rendered into a dance of stag-beetles. (Photo by Archis Achrekar. Courtesy of Centroid Motion Capture and Faceware Technologies.)*

'Frankenstein effect'. 'It should be noted – eyes will follow the body and face will follow emotion, so if they are done separately, there is a lot of work to make it authentic. The best result is P-cap, but facial capture is very frustrating' (David Footman).

There is another frustrating element of facial capture that any cinematics director will have encountered. Even if the capture is good and the animators create something good from the data:

The facial performance doesn't always make it into the game due to (real-time engine) optimisation. In 'Far Cry 5', what we captured compared to what is on screen didn't compare. Film and TV have run ahead. We can't draw the polys or run blend-shapes at run-time. [In comparison] [i]n the recent Marvel Films, Thanos – created by Digital Domain – has incredible subtlety. Games can't do it so well. I've just finished 'Watch Dogs: Legion' and the lip-sync is done procedurally,* whereas from below the nose to the forehead is run by facial captured animation – it's so frustrating.

DAVID FOOTMAN

*What we mean here is that lip-sync can be animated automatically by the waveform of the sound being analysed and then driving the lips to move in sync. As you'll imagine, it doesn't look great, but it saves a lot of time and money!

Working with pre-recorded audio

Working as a teacher, I usually find that actors find this really hard, if not the hardest element of acting in the volume – you have to act to someone else's interpretation of a scene, recorded in a booth and played through a speaker onto the floor for you to play to. Actors who really attempt to bring the words alive, inhabiting the character and speaking the lines out loud – since their audio is not being recorded – seem to do best.

> People with dance or combat experience have an advantage ... those without end up doing the same movements. But whatever your background, wildly creative people hear that little hitch in the voice and find that in their body.
>
> AMERICA YOUNG

> Pre-recorded audio might still happen with smaller Studios. But I'd still record body and audio first and use them as a guide and then ADR* later on.
>
> STEVE KNIEBIHLY

*ADR – automated dialogue replacement – has been used for years in movies. It's time consuming and expensive in terms of actor and studio time, but it means the voice can be the main focus, plus it's possible to also capture the facial performance at the same time. If you are asked to do face and voice at the same time, heed this advice:

> Doing facial ADR is not so different from regular ADR, except you have to get the eyelines right. [Also] [i]t's difficult to get into the rhythm. So know your lines. Voice actors are so used to not caring about their face, but they need to know their lines. Older actors think ADR is easy. Be a hard worker. Learn your lines. Have ideas and make notes.
>
> STEVE KNIEBIHLY

When it hasn't been possible to use a HMC or record voice in an action sequence, more work is required. 'Sometimes I will do a face and voice pass over stunt work, putting in close ups into a stunt scene'

(Steve Kniebihly). A game I worked on required a moment between two characters in the middle of a fight, which was being hand-animated. I was able to facially capture this in two quick shots to be inserted into the scene.

While we are on the subject of voice, we have always had voice actors come to our classes working on the basis that, as they have voiced animated characters, they would like to try to move them too. It doesn't always work out, for reasons Kniebihly expands on here: 'I don't like to work with voice-only actors. If they have been working a lot for some time, they forget that they have a body which is not a good match for a mocap actor' (Steve Kniebihly). I would add – just bear in mind that what we said earlier holds true – the skeleton does not lie!

A practical exercise in working with pre-recorded audio

You can practise working with pre-recorded audio at home. Take a sound recording from a movie or a game and try to act one of the characters out, paying particular attention to their timing, their breath and how their voice suggests their character might move.

When you've memorized the words and can recite them in time with the original, start to work them into your physical performance including gestures, pauses and moments of stillness. You'll find that saying the words yourself will energize your performance. Whenever we mime or mouth words it changes, or inhibits our movement, so I advise you to vocalize in time with the original.

If you can do this well and can inhabit different characters with different rhythms, you are on your way to the skills needed to be a flexible, versatile 'generalist' actor, as David Footman calls it – very valuable for cinematics in the volume.

How does interactivity in a scene affect performance?

As we've been hearing, one of the advantages is that there are generally long takes – sometimes the full scene – allowing actors to really get into a good flow.

> There are, however, a fair number of exceptions to playing a scene in full. Most commonly, this is because physical aspects or stunts require the scene to be broken down into smaller chunks (e.g. if there's a jump from a height that requires its own set up). Additionally, when capturing performance for VR, the player will ordinarily be able to interact at frequent intervals, therefore scenes may need to be broken up into many parts (a new action after each player interaction).
>
> KATE SAXON

Steve Kniebihly expands further:

> In Branching Narrative there are specific challenges – there is a main branch that will split into A+B and rejoin at C. In terms of staging and blocking everything has to be consistent. The actors have to deal with possible totally opposite decisions but still rejoin the same narrative. A – your child dies, B – s/he survives, but you have to make C make sense as the scene continues [with a reaction that covers both events]. You can use the Kuleshov* effect [with a neutral reaction] after a scene – using your edits and juxtaposition of shots to tell the story.
>
> STEVE KNIEBIHLY

*For anyone who is unfamiliar with the Kuleshov effect, this is a film editing (montage) effect demonstrated by Soviet filmmaker Lev

Kuleshov in the 1910s and 1920s. It is a mental phenomenon by which viewers interpret added meaning from the interaction of two sequential shots rather than from a single shot in isolation. It means that meaning is added to a character's neutral expression. For actors and visual storytellers, this was a crucial discovery, which we have used ever since.

> Just reading a branching narrative script can be a nightmare. Actors are used to reading lines on a page. I've found that script reading and lots of rehearsals helps. . . . However this is not always allowed!
>
> STEVE KNIEBIHLY

Then there is the Quicktime event in which the player has to react quickly to get a character out of trouble.

> Say you are playing a character and he suddenly gets strangled by the bad guy. The player has to button mash to survive. The choke has to be on a loop starting and finishing in the matching position so you can't see the join. That technical ability needs to be at the back part of the actor's brain and not affect their performance. Actors who are able to take 4 different notes here are crucial.
>
> STEVE KNIEBIHLY

This is an important point. Often in a mocap shoot there will be multiple notes, some technical and some psychological. My modus operandi as a director is always to minimize my notes to actors, but sometimes it cannot be helped. Actors who can embody their characters believably while at the same time serving the technical needs of the animation and gameplay will be hired again!

Figure 7.5 *Often in a mocap shoot, there will be multiple notes, some technical and some psychological. An actor's ability to be able to process different notes is crucial. (Photo by Archis Achrekar. Courtesy of Centroid Motion Capture.)*

Cameras in cinematics

There are three kinds of cameras used in a line-of-sight optical mocap studio. First, as we've mentioned before, there are the *infra-red* cameras that see the reflectors and capture the points in space that make up the point-cloud in space that represents the skeleton of the character. These will be fixed to the wall or on tripods all around you. They are likely to be glowing red and there will be a lot of them. They are carefully aligned with millimetre precision accuracy, so woe betide anyone who knocks into one, or the supports they are clamped to!

Second, there are *reference* cameras also known as *witness* cameras. Some studios have them fixed in a wide shot so the animation team knows where the sequence is happening in space later on. Sometimes

Figure 7.6 *The infra-red cameras that see the reflectors and capture the points in space that make up the point-cloud in space that represents the skeleton of the character. These will be fixed to the wall or on tripods all around you. (From Centroid Studio. Photo by Archis Achrekar. Courtesy of Centroid Motion Capture and Motion Analysis Corporation.)*

these are designated to different characters and are operated so there is a clear shot for the animator to refer to later. It may be that a gesture is not clear from the data and the reference/witness cam helps to make it clear what the actor was doing. The video shot from these cameras is used as reference – as the name suggests – as a guide for the animators when they work on the fine tuning of the animation.

In the studio, you may well notice four-way split screens, which show reference camera images and maybe real-time rendered characters. Or the real-time image may be on a screen on its own.

Lastly is the *virtual* camera. It acts like a film camera, but *in* the virtual environment. This can be in the form of a digital notepad screen which acts as a virtual camera and can 'see' the digital 3D environment, adjusting accordingly as it moves. We have mentioned

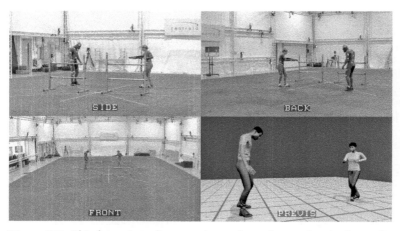

Figure 7.7 *This four-way split screen image from the monitor in the studio shows three different views of the action from reference cameras. Also included is the real-time rendering of the characters on the bottom right. (Photo by Archis Achrekar. Courtesy of Centroid Motion Capture.)*

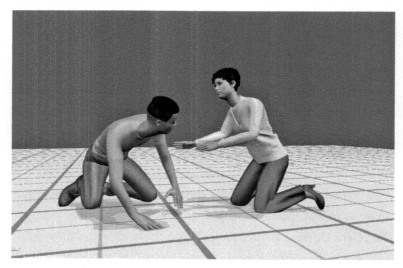

Figure 7.8 *The real-time rendered characters may be on a screen on their own. (Photo by Archis Achrekar. Courtesy of Centroid Motion Capture.)*

how a reflector's position is captured – when it's on an actor's body, it pinpoints where it is in space. If reflectors are attached to a screen or digital camera, likewise the animator knows where the camera is in the space and can be used in real-time as the camera perspective in the scene. This data can be adjusted afterwards, or the camera can be shot later. When I first started working in mocap, it was this flexibility that really blew my mind, 'So I can separate performance from camera? I can decide where to position my cameras *after* the shoot?'

I was in Los Angeles, working on a Microsoft game project. Steven Spielberg was shooting the animated film *Tintin* there at the same time. In a separate studio, he had stages the size of large boxing rings set up where he was shooting the camera – using a virtual camera – *after* shooting the performances. The virtual camera has a notepad-sized screen on which the mocap data is played back, with real-time characters dropped onto the actors' cloud data. Since the virtual camera has reflectors on, the system knows where it is in space in relation to the characters. The camera movement data can be captured while the previously recorded performance data is played back. In a three-dimensional space, you can move around a previously shot scene and make decisions on how you are going to shoot it, after the event. For a director used to having to make camera placement, lenses and movement decisions at the same time as directing the performance, this was a revelation.

Even more on virtual cameras

So, it's possible to shoot the camera for a scene later or it can be done at the same time. There is also the hybrid possibility of putting reflectors onto a video camera and tracking its movement in space so that the video can be used as a reference camera and its position in space can be put into the animation data for later. Some directors like to make their camera decisions live.

> For the most part, cameras are specific, so it's important to show the actors where cameras are when I block the scene. We can shoot the master and coverage at the same time – there is no mechanic to do it in multiple takes. I like to get a master shot and then go in to do specific pick-ups. We have reference cameras to protect ourselves.
>
> DAVID FOOTMAN

One of the things many actors like about mocap is that there is no makeup or costume continuity or re-lighting to worry about. Often you can shoot a scene in its entirety and really concentrate on performance.

For Steve Kniebihly, working in mocap is about freedom. He likes to rely on experience and intuition.

> First of all, you're not as tied to camera placement. If you choose, you can be totally free of blocking. You can set it, but it's a shame because you don't have to. George Lucas was trying to get rid of the camera on the newer *Star Wars* films. If you learn about the freedom of mocap you can take a lot of shortcuts in the volume that you couldn't in TV. 'Fix it in post' is actually true, easier and doesn't necessarily cost. I don't need to set the cameras before – good staging is liberating and then I can work it out later. I can focus on the truth of the scene. I can always find a good angle 99 per cent of the time – only 1 per cent of the time I'm blocked. Setting cameras is one more way to mess up a scene. I don't use the virtual camera on the day. I always do it later on. I record the virtual cameras afterwards, spending time getting it right then.

For myself, I have done it both ways depending on the game, the experience of the animation team and the amount of involvement I have in post-production. There are benefits to doing substantial previsualization. It also depends on the trust the team has in the director.

> Right now in Japan, we do previs. If I were left to myself I wouldn't do it, but previs is good for other departments. I worked on a *Planet of the Apes* interactive film and I did no previs. The more experienced you get, the less you think about things beforehand, the more you let yourself be surprised by what the actor will bring. If you work and are so focused on imagining what will be when you read a script, you don't allow the actors the opportunity to bring surprises. But if I'm not the sole creative authority, then I need to do previs and storyboards for other departments.
>
> STEVE KNIEBIHLY

The virtual camera can be useful for actors to understand how their characters in the setting will look. By looking at the real-time screen, seeing what the virtual camera sees they can get a better idea of what they are capturing:

> A virtual camera is really helpful, as once in the avatar's skin, a simple movement can play out somewhat differently than you might at first imagine. As a basic example, if you're playing a fifteen-foot tall sorceress, she may need to stretch her back out more gracefully when bending to pick something up off the floor, than you might at 5' 6". Also, a game environment is often larger than life in scale, whether that's something as simple as the size of a table or something more magnificent, such as a magical forest. So seeing your avatar moving in that space, or interacting with that furniture, can inform decisions as to how to most suitably move in order to fit in seamlessly.
>
> KATE SAXON

Yuji Shimomura agrees – 'I tend to fix the cameras afterwards and use the virtual camera only to share the world with the actors.'

On the other hand, it may be that, in your cinematic, the player can decide where to see the action. In which case you need to know that and ensure that your performance will read wherever it is seen from. Here your theatre in the round skills will come into play and you'll need to know not only in which direction the player may be, but also how close. There is no point giving your best wide shot performance when the player could see you right up close.

Remember to ask the director about cameras – we all know how important it is to know where your performance is going to be seen from. 'To the actor: act like the camera is always on you – it could be a close up, it could be a master shot. Everyone has to be in the moment the whole time. One hundred per cent of the time – even if there are three characters and you have one line. I still want you to react' (Steve Kniebihly).

The vibe in a mocap studio

The crew in the mocap studio is likely to be considerably smaller than on a film or TV set. There are no sparks, makeup, costume etc. needed. The scenery and props department is minimal and may be run by runners, floor assistants or assistant directors. It's also a less hierarchical and more collaborative medium, so you *may* find there are fewer egos around! The jobs that people are doing are probably more technical and computer based, because of the digital medium and complex data pipelines required.

America Young is very positive about working as a woman in games:

In mocap I've experienced the least amount of misogyny, compared to film and TV. Even though when I started the content of the games were mostly about my character being captured or saved. Though there was inherent misogyny in the game, the people were phenomenal – supportive, kind, collaborative. In *Saints Row* I had to do a pole dance, but the team was amazing. Now the content has changed a bit – female characters are much more kick-ass – but I'm happy to say I can't think of any game where I felt uncomfortable.

AMERICA YOUNG

If that gives you a positive feeling it should, because video games are changing. When I first started out there were few roles for females, but things are changing fast. America Young again when I asked her if things were getting better:

Maybe. The game I'm working on at the moment is the closest to parity so far. More women are on the team – there is around 50/50 women to men in the room. The world is finally seeing how many women out there are gamers. Women are voting with their dollars. This brings with it financial power, with women moving up the ranks. Many men like playing female characters – most guys aren't creeps – they want to see change too in content.

AMERICA YOUNG

Kate Saxon echoes Young here:

I've come across very little sexism in terms of how I've been treated in games. Generally, I've found it a respectful environment. However, historically, many female games characters were penned as nothing more than sexist fantasies of women, rather than realistic, flawed and complex beings. The industry has made considerable progress in addressing this, and some games are creating fantastic roles for women nowadays.

KATE SAXON

The key for Steve Kniebihly is to get the right people in the room:

> There was a time when you needed to have one actor do ten things.
> But that's more specific to animations. But for cinematics you're
> looking for great actors. However, one of the things you want to
> avoid is having a bad apple, an asshole, on the set. You get better
> results if there is a good vibe on set. Just be nice. Just be a decent
> person. It is so important to try and build a good feel on set. Once
> you realise that it's OK not to have the answer and rely on the team
> to come up with an answer you can be more relaxed, more flexible,
> finding solutions. There are many cooks.
>
> STEVE KNIEBIHLY

I can only echo what these three directors have said here and
emphasize the notion that there is little room for big and imposing
egos in a mocap studio. In fact, it meant that when I returned recently
to the live action set and encountered an aggressive and macho special
effects supervisor in the midst of a night shoot, it made me wish I was
instead back in the volume working with a smaller group of
collaborators with less masculine pride being thrown around.

Keeping character continuity over the shooting schedule

As we outlined in the animation chapter, video games development
cycles and shooting schedules are unlike film and television. They ebb
and flow between 'vertical slices' (a section of the game produced for the
publisher as a proof of concept) and phases of production. For film and
television actors, shooting out of narrative sequence is common, but
imagine shooting sporadically, with weeks or months in between shoots.
Maintaining character continuity – physically, vocally and psychologically

– can be a challenge. Performers will be expected to get back into the role(s) very quickly, even after an extended break, so asking animators for video and in-game clips will be crucial as reference.

If actors are not available, there may be no alternative but to recast. Then, as a new actor you have an even bigger challenge – to fill the role of a character whose performance has already been captured by another actor. If that is the case, watching previously shot material is essential, as well as thorough discussions with animators and directors in terms of what they need, how the previous actor moved and how they played their scenes.

Chapter 7 takeaways

Directing cinematics is different from other media	The performance director's position and status in the process varies in different projects.
What are cinematics?	cinematics are dramatic scenes and the stakes are always high, interactivity is key and the relationship with the player crucial.
How are cinematics created?	Whether prescriptive in terms of fulfilling previs, or more freeing, the performer needs to deliver what the animator and director need.
A note on preparation	Whether you have rehearsal time or no time at all to prepare, or NDAs hamper information flow, flexibility is key.
Mocap, facial capture, performance capture and working with pre-recorded audio	With an understanding of the many different permutations of capture and why and when they occur – which can create the 'Frankenstein effect' – you will have a better idea of how to modulate your performance. Acting to someone else's voice can be surprisingly inspiring.
How does interaction in a scene affect performance?	Understanding the player's interaction in a scene and the needs of the game developers to support gameplay will help you deliver in the volume.

Cameras in cinematics	There are different cameras that you will encounter in the volume – infra-red, reference/witness and virtual cameras. The virtual camera can free things up and can separate the performance from the camera.
The vibe in a mocap studio	It is very different to work in a mocap studio compared with film and stage. There tends to be more gender equality, and collaborative and ego-free behaviour is both valued and expected.

8

Direction and the lack of it

JOHN DOWER

This chapter will outline the reality of what actors are frequently confronted by in the volume. How actors are booked, contracted and directed is often a surprise, since the games industry in particular does not always put the actor at the centre of the process. The actor is part of the team, and understanding their role as a collaborator is essential. Mocap shoots are sometimes run by animators who know what they want but do not have the directing experience to communicate it to the actor, and the needs of an interactive narrative are often at odds with clear linear character development. Here we listen to performers who give you realistic tools to self-direct if needed and to interpret result-oriented direction if you are given it. We will encourage you to develop an attitude to become more independent than you may be used to, if required.

Contributors – Kezia Burrows (actor in mocap), Richard Dorton (actor, USA casting director, director, mocap teacher for The Mocap Vaults) and Jessica Jefferies (casting director).

Expectations of a director

Many of you will have experienced being directed by a variety of different directors with different styles and approaches. You may have become used to weeks of rehearsal for a play, much of this time being spent on script analysis. Perhaps you have worked more on physicality, less on dialogue. Conversely, you may have worked in film and done very little rehearsal but prepared yourself in advance with a script. Then, once on set, you may have encountered an actor-friendly director or maybe a director who appears to have little interest in you and is more interested in the staging and shots. Directors come in many different shapes and sizes.

So, what is it that a director does? I would define the job this way – they are the representative of the audience/player in the studio/set. They see the scene from the player's or audience's perspective and make sure that the story is told to the viewer. No-one else has that specific job on a film set, or on stage. However, when it comes to games, it could be argued that the games designer and the animator also have that job. It's not a huge surprise therefore that sometimes they see the performance director either as superfluous or peripheral and the animator is tasked with directing.

This works fine if the animator is used to working with actors and has empathy with what they need. However, often animators have had little experience working with actors except maybe in the sound booth, which means they can be anything from intimidated to ignorant about what actors need. Whenever I train animators to work in mocap, I stress the need to think about what the actor needs to help them create a great performance, not necessarily just what the animator needs from the actor. However, there will be times when you are confronted by someone who doesn't know how to help and inspire you and you may need to self-direct.

Let's go back to my definition above. If you are to be the director, it's up to you to think about what the viewer is going to experience. You have to be actor and audience at the same time! How do you do that? Let's hear from some actors with experience in mocap on how they deal with this challenge.

The different types of mocap work

There are quite a few skills needed from directors working in mocap and they are rarely found in the same person. When I asked Richard Dorton about his different experiences of being directed in mocap, he was keen to start on the subject by emphasizing the difference between in-game and cinematics.

> For cinematics – this still varies depending on the studio. Studios will bring in actors earlier, give out the script earlier, give rehearsal time and time needed to know the story. Smaller Studios try to do it on the day. In this case being able to improv and work fast come into play. When you are working in-game you are dealing with an animation director. They hire combat specific directors – for example in martial arts, fighting etc. who understand moves for a game. It's a separate world. Not a lot of people do both cinematics and in-game. The pressure to find a better actor is at stake, plus multiple shoots means often there are two teams working separately on the same game at the same time.
>
> RICHARD DORTON

So, it's not just about having a director or not, but perhaps different kinds of director – with specific skills whether in for example – combat, martial arts, animation or maybe drama only. Regarding drama,

> There are directors coming in from TV, film and theatre who can find the medium challenging. They have to do what the animator or studio requires and are limited with their creative direction within the time frame. There's an element of learning and adapting their skills on the job to translate that to the actor for a fully lived-in performance beyond just the physicality.
>
> KEZIA BURROWS

So, you may find yourself being directed by someone who knows how to work with actors, but not so much about the specific needs of the medium. Given it's a fast-evolving medium in the first decades from coming into being, it's not surprising that there is a lot of change and few directors with good, rounded experience of the needs of technology, gameplay and animation.

While we're on the theme of the multiple aspects of mocap that may challenge you and the director, there is also the reality of working on several projects at the same time, each with different demands.

> I'm currently working on three performance capture projects at the moment, seven voice projects and occasionally body mocap only. On two projects they're also using my likeness, voice and body. For *Star Citizen* and *Alien Isolation*, they used my likeness [however] fundamentally it's all acting. My approach is the same, but what's different are the technical aspects and the differences in the environments. The skill is applying your acting techniques and keeping that authentic performance. It's still coming from a real

place but your body speaks more. Some actors find it hard to think from the body in. I use Stanislavski and Laban – who am I, etc.

KEZIA BURROWS

What's interesting about what Kezia is saying here is that she has many projects on the go at the same time, filming a day or a few days here on one, then moving to another and so on. Maintaining character continuity and focus while shooting, quite possibly out of sequence, in an erratic and perhaps unpredictable schedule is hard enough; doing that sometimes without the support of a performance director is even harder. That's where self-reliance and your own good practice will pay dividends. More on this later.

What kind of information do you get before arriving at the studio?

First up, let's hear from a casting director about their perspective. Jessica Jefferies has been casting mocap jobs for a while now, having previously been a mocap actor.

> In terms of casting, I need to know as much detail as possible in order to cast. This has got better – I know what I need so I ask for it. I need to know the soul and backbone of the characters. My aim is to try and get into the creative's heads. I talk to writers, game designers, performance directors and game directors. When on a call with all of them they can find differences in opinion. Conversations early on are important. I need some form of script and an idea of what kind of language and dialogue the characters use. We try to come to some kind of consensus and translate the games developers' terminology into something usable for performance.

JESSICA JEFFERIES

It's important to stress here that for a games developer to go to the trouble and expense of hiring a casting director, they must be of a certain size and standard. It's pleasing to be able to say that it's becoming more and more usual for a casting process to take place that we would recognize from film and TV. However, it's still less likely to happen for lower budget jobs and even less for in-game animation.

> In the past there was a smaller group of people doing mocap. Smaller companies would contact you and say can you come in to do these couple of days. Mocap acting is often independent of an agent, whereas performance capture is often cast – done from self tapes or in person.
>
> KEZIA BURROWS

When you get to the studio, you may have been trusted with script and character breakdowns or you may get the information on the day. Whatever the case, NDAs will have been signed and much secrecy observed. Hopefully not to the extent of the James Bond example I gave in the previous chapter but expect not to be allowed to discuss the job outside the studio. As we've made clear before, you need to know what *you* need to perform well and ask for it, especially if it's not clear from the script.

> If there is no real character development you have to be present and ask the essential questions. I have to know where I have come from. I love some back story in order to give me clarity and confidence with the character as a reason for making choices. It helps offer up new ideas both internally and physically to understand the life before the scene.
>
> KEZIA BURROWS

We have previously covered in detail the challenges of working with the body, working in imaginary environments and creating a character. Use the advice, tips and exercises to make sure you are as prepared as you can be to work quickly and to know what it is you need to create great work.

How often are you directed by what you would call a director?

As you'd expect from what I've outlined above, you won't be meeting directors of the calibre of David Footman, Steve Kniebihly or Kate Saxon at every mocap booking. What do you do if not? Are we seeing an appreciation as to what performance directors do?

It happens less and less these days that there isn't a performance director involved, which might be more about the types of project I am working on. This is probably more about the level of the projects and the fact they understand the value of a director – these are likely to be games which are more character and narrative driven. If there isn't a performance director there may be many voices in the volume. A really good director will tap into the best way to bring out the actor and translate the technical language for them, but if there is not a director the voices are coming directly from the technical team. The emphasis is not on character and emotion and drive through a scene, but more on technical movements, blocking and not so character-driven. When I was an actor, I had to direct myself often. In this situation it's best if actors collaborate and you become very good at having an outside eye. I used the real-time screens and my knowledge of the technology and games. However, it's best if there is a director since otherwise there is too much to think about.

JESSICA JEFFERIES

Jessica's observations regarding the technical team tap into what we have described regarding performance capture, which comes with as many technical expectations as there are technicians responsible for mocap, facial capture, voice recording etc. Here you'll be expected to be able to take multiple technical and blocking notes as well as character notes.

But what if there is a director who really doesn't know how to help the performer, who sees things from the perspective of what they need but not what the actor needs? As in this situation in any acting medium, it's up to the performer to use all of their psychological skills – empathy, curiosity and emotional intelligence as well as their acting skills and experience. To some extent, you could see it as having to do other people's work for them, but you could also view it as a chance to exercise your generosity and collaborative skills. Motion capture offers technical challenges as well as interpersonal ones and here is a good example of an actor who is open-minded enough to appreciate this:

> If you have a director who is not used to working with actors, it's important to know when to go with it or offer up something from your experience. Sometimes you can do both, which is ideal – take their meaning and apply it to the mocap, but communication is always very important. It's a learning curve for everyone. I use my experience but it's such an evolving technology, it's important to stay adaptable and leave your ego at the door. I've had the experience of being overloaded with information – getting notes from directors and animators. I have eleven years in the volume and I will try to be the actor and the director if necessary. I go with what I've learnt. I'll hear what the games tech specialists need – for example turn the wheel faster etc. I'll listen to what has to happen from the game design perspective. Then I'll make sure the breath is

working and I'll make a considered choice with the physicality and play the intention – but remembering it's really important to hit the marks of what the games developers need. It's also ok to get it wrong – every choice gives a place to work from, e.g. more, less, stronger, weaker, right, wrong. When directors are experienced and understand both actors and the gaming world it is easier, making it more creative, freeing and fun. You need mutual trust and an outside eye. If there isn't a director there then I need to see playback and be my own outside eye.

KEZIA BURROWS

I am struck by how Kezia's intuitive can-do team-working attitude is as much to do with her success as her talent as an actor. In fact, they are frequently intertwined.

Regarding the issue of a director being absent, I suspect that this is going to be even more the case after the reality of Covid has sunk in and we have started to get used to not always being in the same room. Digital technology is allowing us to work remotely and this is happening for shoots too. It may be that you will have the director watching remotely, with their direction being translated from another language or at least interpreted by someone in the room.

Kezia describes working on a scene while being directed remotely:

I worked on a project where we would run a scene – running up some stairs and seeing a landscape beyond being destroyed. Then there was a ten-minute delay and then we were told to do it at half the speed and put your left hand down before the right. They looked at the 3D environment to make blocking work but at this point there were no performance notes. I wanted to ask questions that would inform the character choices – for example, where is the sun? Do I see people die? Do I know any of the people who are dying? They knew the answers and were happy to share, but they weren't a director so didn't know to offer it. When you have the pre-recorded audio to work with in these situations, it can make it easier.

KEZIA BURROWS

Again, in situations like this, an ability and positive attitude to self-direct are essential. Let's develop that thought.

What do you do if the direction is confusing, not useful or non-existent?

Once an animator wanted me to do a stunt that was not physically possible. I pointed out that I could only do what was physically possible!! It can be a weird balance when you are discovering and creating together – in that case we were both directing! Another time, an animator's direction was – 'you're going to stand in a base pose, then do some acting, then come back to the idle'! He thought it was my job to fill in the blanks! Another situation in which your character might be asked to do contradictory things is in a branching narrative game, as in the player has options and different responses. You can be in a situation where you feel as though your character wouldn't do that or react like that, but gameplay has dictated that the option should be available even if it would be something unnatural for the character.

JESSICA JEFFERIES

We touched on this issue in the previous chapter, when describing the challenges presented by branching narratives and how the character might have to revert to a predetermined option which works despite significantly different events happening previously due to player choices (see references to the Kuleshov effect in Chapter 7).

As we all know, directors come in many shapes, sizes and styles in all performance media, so getting unplayable direction is not unique to mocap. All you can do is do your best, make brave and bold choices and hope for the best that they are good ones. Use your communication skills: 'I always fall back on communication. Ask questions, clarify for yourself – you are not wasting time. Just be clear about what is wanted. There is no point in wasting a take if you are not sure' (Jessica Jefferies).

Richard Dorton takes this a stage further – 'if direction contradicts what you believe should work, you need to show them. Often directors know what they don't want but not what they do want. You should say let me show you what works and what doesn't'. Both Jessica and Richard show a lot of confidence and strength of character from their experiences and you'll do well to take their advice and be prepared to stick your neck out if you feel you can offer something better than is being asked for, expected or presumed.

Remember one thing – even if the direction is lacking, you should never use that as an excuse to underperform. In a TV or film show your performance will be being scrutinized by the commissioners, producers and executive producers and in theatre you'll be getting feedback from the audience and reviewers. Similarly, there will be plenty of people judging your performance in mocap. We've heard from animators previously in terms of the extra work they will have to do if the data is below par and you can be sure the animator and games directors will be scrutinizing your performance once in the pipeline. You have to give it your all, in whatever circumstance. One hundred per cent commitment is the expectation, whoever is directing.

Can pre-recorded voice help?

As Kezia has said previously, having a character's voice as a guide can make things clearer, particularly when there is little to go on from the director. At least then there is a clear steer on a crucial aspect of the character. Many character decisions can flow from hearing the voice.

When you have the voice-over to work with in these situations, it can make it easier. If someone else is doing the voice, I put my ego aside. I need to fit my body to the voice. There is no other job where you share a character. When I was doing *007 Legends* there were film references – e.g. Halle Berry and Diana Rigg. I like to start from the feet up and the voice helps you know how they stand. Their rhythm is crucial – sometimes you have to go against your instincts. You need to hear it back as much as possible. Sometimes you'll find yourself playing characters similarly but do not worry as they will look different. It's really helpful to look at the screen since some characters move differently with their costumes.

KEZIA BURROWS

As cinematic director of the game, I remember Kezia's focus and determination to do these voices justice. We didn't always use the original Bond cast members since they were not always available and, if that was the case, the voice actor too tried to inhabit the original character's sound and vocal patterns. On the floor, using film references and videos, Kezia worked to be true to that character and I gave her as much time to prepare and rehearse as was possible. Having directed voice actors, I know how important stance, posture and physicality are in creating the sound of the voice. Being mindful of this in the mocap studio makes total sense to me and should be part of the mocap actor's toolbox.

An exercise using pre-recorded audio

Here's an exercise you could use which builds on the one in the previous chapter for pre-recorded audio.

Find a voice only clip that is a good example of an actor you admire. Really listen to it a few times. Ignore the video, just focus on the voice. Find the place where the voice comes from – chest, stomach, diaphragm. Analyse the breath. Were they standing or sitting, walking or moving? Now try to recreate what you imagine was their movement, their stance, their breath as they said these words.

As Kezia says, 'there is no other job where you share a character'. Here's your chance to try it for yourself.

What advice would you have liked when you started out in mocap?

While I accept that things have changed in the industry since these performers started out, I felt it instructive to ask them how things have changed and what it has taught them about what is important for them in creating a quality performance.

> I started acting in mocap in 2010. My early jobs were with veterans and I learnt from them. I was in a very lucky position. I wish I had had all that success and learning curves but in an industry that respected actors and treated them with contracts, understanding and knew what they needed. I wish that there were proper directors and the agents were respected.
>
> JESSICA JEFFERIES

Well, that has really started to change. The success of VFX-driven TV shows, the cross-over success of real-time engines into film and the participation of movie stars in video games has forced games developers to treat acting talent better and to bring better direction into the studio. Along with it, agents and casting directors are becoming the norm. We hope if this book ever gets updated that this chapter will not be necessary.

> I wish performance capture was brought to attention earlier. games were ahead of their time but not until *Polar Express* did we

get a star – Tom Hanks – who demanded we take it more seriously. We never got a whole script. I wish the in-game was taken as seriously as performance capture. Every move is a performance. I'd rather it was called performance capture not mocap – even if you are turning a doorknob it should be as that character.

RICHARD DORTON

We still have a way to go here, but as animation and performance direction converge, there is great hope for a future where the importance and the quality of the performance is elevated, and dramatic cinematic performance, embodiment of character, stunt work and in-game characterization are given equal weight by all concerned.

Take it seriously! It's proper acting! Even if you're not playing the full character it's a facet of this being that needs full investment. Often, we will be off script performing it as a whole, even though the body will be the only part of the mocap performance used. The Laban technique is a great foundation if you're working in the unknown – it allows quick intuitive choices. I'm thankful for my acting training and the tools it gave me to assist in these choices. Remember – you're the actor, you're there to do what you do – be confident in that. It's a unique environment with lots of plusses. Be kind and easy to work with – people will want to work with you again.

KEZIA BURROWS

This echoes what so many people have said in the book, and absolutely echoes my own experience of the industry. Having worked with my fair share of ego-fuelled 'talent' and been at the receiving end of some *interesting* behaviour verging on the abusive – particularly in TV – I have got to the stage where I value true collaboration highly and pure naked ambition much less so. Be someone the crew looks forward to working with – today, tomorrow and in the future.

As Kezia adds: 'It's important to remember how long people have worked on a project before you arrive. I'm a part of a game that could have cost millions. Learn more about how it works, how the suits work – calibration, why you have the dots, learn the technology. Never stop learning!' It doesn't surprise me that Kezia is asked back to work again and again. She takes it seriously, works hard, does her prep and research and is fun to work with as a collaborator. She's an inspiration.

And here is the secret!

You can never do the job hungover! You need to be as fresh and alert as you can be. Do yoga, sleep well, have a coffee and water – whatever you need to be alert, centred and grounded. As long as I have done that, I can only do what I can do. You have to be forgiving, especially if you're a perfectionist. I sometimes have to remind myself that just because you feel you could do a better take, if they are happy with it, you did your job, it works – like any other medium.

KEZIA BURROWS

This chapter has been all about encouraging independence and collaboration. It's not an ideal solution for an actor trying to do a good job, but it is sometimes realistic. If the job of the director is to be the audience's representative in the room, then if they are partially or wholly absent then the actor has to fill the gaps. Staying alert, collaborative and willing to be flexible is essential if this happens. In mocap, animators who understand the needs of the performer and performance directors are becoming more common. Even so, developing the many collaborative skills mentioned in this chapter will stand the performer in good stead and prepare them for the challenges ahead.

Chapter 8 takeaways

Expectations of the director	The director's job is to be the representative of the viewer/payer or audience. If they are not present, this becomes your responsibility.
The different types of mocap work	There are many different types of director you will encounter in mocap. You'll likely be working on several projects over a long time. Self-reliance, 100 per cent commitment, good organization and practice are essential.
What kind of information do you get before arriving at the studio?	While the amount of information you get prior to a mocap shoot varies, your preparedness and knowing what information you yourself need to work quickly will help to deal with the challenge.
How often are you directed by a director?	By developing a strong outside eye and understanding the perspective of the viewer, you will increase independence and deliver better performances.
More on working with pre-recorded voice	Actors can use pre-recorded voice as inspiration, including an exercise where you can try to recreate a performance of an actor you admire.
How has mocap changed?	The status of performers in mocap has changed significantly for the better. Maintaining a positive attitude will help you become more employable.

9

The industry – finding your place in a new medium

JOHN DOWER

Capture technology is now used in games, education, film and theatre. The majority of capture work is currently in game development. Access to mocap work varies from one territory to another, although they share common obstacles. In this chapter we interview experienced actors, casting directors and mocap experts from all over the world, who can shed light on what can appear to be a confusing and opaque process. Readers will learn tips on further training, how to be ready when opportunity knocks and how to let the world know.

Contributors – Jessica Jefferies (casting director), Richard Dorton (actor, USA casting director, director, mocap teacher for The Mocap Vaults), Kezia Burrows (actor in mocap), Kate Saxon (theatre, television and cinematics director), Bryan Steagall (animator and distributor for OptiTrack, Stretchsense and Rokoko at Kidskorner), Mari Ueda and Kumiko Ogawa (mocap producers at Pivot Motion Inc.), Steve Kniebihly (cinematics director), Yuji Shimomura (action and cinematics director) and Jeasy Seghal (mocap and virtual production producer, consultant and trainer at Graphic Monk).

Mocap is proving its worth

I started writing this chapter on the day that *Variety* published an article on 'The Top 10 Best Motion Capture Performances on Film'.[1] It states that 'motion capture is extremely difficult, but the entertainment industry at large hasn't fully embraced its place in the medium, often paying the actors much less and no major awards body recognizing it as its own category'. To me, just the fact that this is being debated and that the actor's place in the composite performance is being recognized and prized so highly just shows how far we have come in the last two decades since Andy Serkis's Gollum hit our screens. Indeed, perhaps predictably, Serkis's performance as Gollum/Sméagol from the film *The Lord of the Rings: The Two Towers* (2002) is at the number one spot in *Variety*'s list.

Since then, Serkis has caused controversy with his claims for ownership of the mocapped performance and Spielberg's infamous quote that the post work is simply a matter of 'digital makeup' didn't go down so well with animators, but there is no denying the intense debate among critics and the appreciation from audiences for these digitally created characters has elevated their relevance and appreciation. Indeed, as *Variety* points out:

> Serkis has had mild attempts of breaking through; he was given a special digital acting performance award at the Critics Choice

Awards for his turn as Gollum in 'The Lord of the Rings: The Two Towers' (2002). Nearly a decade later, he was thrust into the Oscar conversation when he picked up a best supporting actor nomination for his work as Caesar, the evolved chimpanzee in Rupert Wyatt's invigorating 'Rise of the Planet of the Apes' (2011). Finding recognition alongside the likes of Kenneth Branagh ('My Week with Marilyn'), Nick Nolte ('Warrior') and eventual winner Christopher Plummer ('Beginners'), his nom marks the first and only major recognition for the acting art form.[2]

As this book has argued, this is a medium that is here to stay, and the success of the films *Variety* lists here is a testament to the power of well-acted and executed motion captured performances.

So how about you? How do you find your place in this new medium? There are no easy answers, but we want to paint a picture of where the industry is at now, which will give you a clearer idea of the opportunities out there. I've spoken to a host of people around the world about this and there follows a host of different perspectives.

How has the industry changed in your part of the world?

I start with this question since we'll get quickly to a sense of perspective on how the past affects the future and continues to do so. Let's start with this positive statement from UK casting director Jessica Jefferies:

The industry has changed massively since 2010. There is completely different technology. I'm now working in VR, different types of scanning, new mocap technology, volumetric capture, mixed media, television and games. Games are becoming more sophisticated – there are strong female roles, BAME characters, richer stories and the industry is opening up to new talent. Regarding sexism, there were often no other women involved in the shoots when I started out. No technicians, no games developers, and few characters – I'd often cover all of them. Now there are producers, production managers, tech people behind the desks, designers, directors and many more female characters.

We hear this experience both echoed and developed by an actor:

It's more open to people, other actors. It's more detailed, more narratively and technically advanced which means we can be more specific and less exaggerated compared to say, 2009. There is more respect – I don't have to convince other people that it is acting so often! Regarding sexism in games, when I started it was very physical and there was a lot of combat. There were instances of basic stage combat being directed for me by untrained male actors who assumed I wouldn't know, even though I'd studied it and was certified. There seemed to be an unconscious bias at times in that regard. This is now rare. Before I would stay quiet and let the work speak, but now I would respectfully address it. Communication is always better for everyone. On one occasion doing a mocap love scene, the male took the reins without discussion – there was no director as such as we were being directed remotely with a translator. I had to tread carefully to be respectful, whilst also communicating the best course of action from past experiences with these scenes. Whether this was to do with my gender or just potential nerves from the other actor, either way it's my responsibility to be bold and communicate in those moments. As I said before, it's rare and becoming rarer. I've had mostly great experiences with male performers in this situation. Now, animators and developers often give a PowerPoint presentation of the game, the world and the characters before we start the job. I've noticed over the years the change and growth, with less needless sexualisation of the female characters. There are a lot more of them – most characters could be a man or a woman, which also helps with equality, plus there is more emphasis on LGBTQ themes and characters.

KEZIA BURROWS

In 2014, when we started teaching acting for motion capture, we would often have up to half the class made up of female performers and it was hard to suggest there was much work for them. That has really changed in the intervening years and there is a real sense of parity between the genders when it comes to casting.

In Australasia, there has been another inspiration in the world of motion capture – this time coming from high-end production.

In the last five years, in film particularly, things have developed with Weta Digital having produced *Avatar* and with *Avatar 2* currently being produced. The trickle-down effect is there but it's mostly high-end. The knowledge basket and toolset has grown however. The games industry is booming with almost a billion dollars in exports.

JEASY SEGHAL

We'll hear more from Jeasy later in terms of how this boom in high-end film production has affected the local industries.

In Latin America, opportunities have begun to open up too:

As an animator, I thought that motion capture would be a more automatic tool into animation. I have had a relationship with Latin America from the beginning and immediately saw OptiTrack as an opportunity for Mexico and expanded in Latin America – not just mocap for animation and movies but also by biomechanics.

BRYAN STEAGALL

The picture Bryan paints of the situation in Latin America is not easy, as we will outline later, but the opportunities are there, as we will see.

Where are we now? Where is the work?

We've already debunked the notion that performing in mocap might be easier due to the fact it captures only the skeleton. Ten years ago, there was a relatively small staple of performers getting most of the work but that has changed and now there is as much competition as in other media. There is lots more work, but there are a lot more people wanting to do it.

> It is not easier to get work nowadays. There are more opportunities but the acting industry is as competitive as it always was. For an actor it can feel there is no rhyme or reason. There are more casting directors and performance directors and more openness to new talent, but what matters is being best for the role.
>
> JESSICA JEFFERIES

In the United States, the picture is the same:

> There is more competition. Mocap is just another medium now. Actors are actors and should be able to work in all mediums. Those who discounted it before now want to work in it – for example Samuel L. Jackson now wants to do mocap on a game – not just the voice as he did on GTA.
>
> RICHARD DORTON

In Japan, mocap is also being used in another way, which points to easier access and might attract the more entrepreneurial:

> There are less mocap stages in Japan. However, there is the phenomenon of VTubers. Using basic mocap – masks, celebrity,

tech and anonymity – helping you to be who you want to be. Examples include – KIZUNA AI, KAGUYA LUNA and MARAI AKARI. Most of them use Oculus and HTC Vive. Facerig [which became available in 2015] on Steam.

MARI UEDA and KUMIKO OGAWA

It is fascinating that cultural attitudes to anonymity and celebrity, coupled with theatrical traditions that favour mask work, have helped to create this trend. *Virtual YouTubers* or *VTubers* originated in Japan in the mid-2010s. The majority of VTubers are Japanese-speaking YouTubers or live-streamers who use anime-inspired avatar designs. By 2020, there were more than 10,000 active VTubers. While it's logical perhaps that the technology has been embraced in Japan, the fact that it is being used and developed domestically means there are opportunities outside of the mainstream games and film industries.

In New Zealand there is a mixed picture, both in terms of opportunities and training.

The government has got behind this. There is lots of investing, but there is a big gap between the elite who are at the top of the food chain to the studios and smaller production companies beneath. Education is trying to fill the gap with courses and funding – both technical and creative. However, it's not at the pace it should be. In Auckland there are a number of acting programmes teaching acting and voice acting – but still mostly theatre and film. A handful of institutes use international teachers but mocap training is rare. The big productions are bringing their own crew and cast A-List Hollywood Talent. It's exciting but frustrating at the same time.

JEASY SEGHAL

The opportunities for training in mocap performance are at early stages in most of the world, with drama and acting schools particularly behind the times when it comes to the whole notion of digital performance, animation and even voice work. I'm also sorry to report that the same is true for film schools, though many are beginning to wake up and realize film and TV production is changing. This change is both significant and fast – digital production and real-time engines are here to stay, necessitating new skills, knowledge and approaches. The more nimble independent companies are starting to provide training and mentoring, but the education is patchy in terms of its response to the new digital world.

While New Zealand attempts to capitalize on the Hollywood juggernauts of *The Lord of the Rings* and *Avatar*, which were either shot there or use Weta's expertise,

> Australia is slightly ahead. There are more setups, more international funding and each state in Australia runs independently whereas in New Zealand, it's one big machine over two islands. Before Weta, New Zealand was really only known for extras and support, but since then Hollywood has realised what potential there is here.
>
> JEASY SEGHAL

As hinted at above, the story in Latin America is more challenging.

> Mocap in Latin America is still very much a new industry. The reason it hasn't grown and why it is still in its infancy is the cost. Even though OptiTrack is cheap, compared to the cost of living it is still a huge expense. In the last few years inertial systems and cheaper optical system are being adopted more easily and it's democratised it. There is a shift of trying to acquire the optical systems for industries like robotics and mechanics which are the two major uses of mocap in Latin America. Mocap is not used so much in films – more in games. They are being purchased by games developers themselves since there are no independent studios yet. However, knowledge is

expanding things. Virtual production using real-time engines (Unreal mostly) is a game-changer. 'The Mandalorian' is a big catalyst. Unreal is driving influencers and small-scale Productions. Cost is a major reason. It's difficult to persuade a company to spend $7,000 on a Stretchsense pair of gloves when an animator is paid around $1,000 a month. Why would an animation studio pay that much for mocap gloves when it cost so little to animate by hand? Most animations are very much 2D although there is 3D coming, particularly in Colombia and Mexico but often animators who are trained will go to the US, Canada and Europe.

BRYAN STEAGALL

The brain-drain resulting from the lack of funding and being near to the United States causes Steagall concern, but there is room for optimism: 'Rokoko [Inertial capture] are enabling some really interesting projects and there is the explosion of individual creative projects. Covid has enabled remote creative projects to happen' (Bryan Steagall). So here, mocap is happening at an individual and small start-up level, which means the opportunities for creatives and actors are less organized or advertised.

Green shoots in New Zealand are appearing, too:

The main opportunities are in games and animation. VR and AR are being encouraged by the education sector. Animation and games are being encouraged for start-ups and independent companies. There's not much funding, but if you're lucky there is seed funding and there is also a push by Epic Games via their 'Megagrants' and also by Unity. Megagrants have also come to some education institutions. WETA group have a new CEO and wants to encourage creativity via their creative Talent internship programme for VFX and post production – doors are opening.

JEASY SEGHAL

We've talked a lot in this book about games and other screen media, but there are also opportunities growing in live performance. Pascal has appeared in two theatre productions using motion and facial capture. Perhaps the best known theatre productions with elements of mocap were *The Tempest* and *Dream* by the RSC (Royal Shakespeare Company). (More on this in the next chapter.) Industrial Light and Magic's (ILM) ABBA 'Voyage' show is using mocap to recreate the members of ABBA on stage as holographic avatars as they looked forty years ago! Theatrical experiences utilizing mocap will undoubtedly increase in years to come.

As you can see, the picture is mixed worldwide: the United States, Canada and Europe with arguably the most developed mocap industries. This goes for training too, where there is a nascent community of training companies, even if drama and film schools are still playing catch up. Let's get on to how this affects actors and performers wanting to get their foot in the door.

So how do we find work?

We need to lay out some honest and realistic markers here. We've spent a lot of this book emphasising the unique requirements of acting for mocap, so you wouldn't expect – we hope – that getting into the studio would be anything other than a challenge.

I'm going to open this conversation with my interviewees by a distinctly downbeat view from Latin America:

> My goal with the mocap summit Mexico 2018 [where Pascal and I were teachers] was to gain experience for Mexico. There is not any focus at all on acting for motion capture. Games companies don't think about it. Some actors have gone to the States and Vancouver. It's a hard industry in Latin America to get into. Talent tends to

leave the country. The standard is too low with the way it's run. VFX and 3D artists tend to end up at Pixar and Disney etc. There is a feeling that there is no real industry for actors. Peru, Colombia, Argentina are the same.

BRYAN STEAGALL

Even when it comes to casting for existing projects:

There is not much casting happening – people who are passing by are grabbed by animators! At Centro University, Mexico City, they put more emphasis on animation over film. Columbia has a progressive 3D industry. The government was specific to promote educational games, and VR. In Argentina there is work being done in Buenos Aires and in Brazil, TV Global uses virtual production.

BRYAN STEAGALL

Bryan's view seems to suggest pessimism or at least resignation. He adds: 'There is a fear of technology. The people who have the money, who make the decisions, are mostly running universities and are often older, while the younger people have the interest.'

Ever the optimist, I'm going to take the positives here. It's never going to be the older and more established figures who are going to be the progressives and embrace new technology – that must come from the younger generation. That has become clear to me over the years I have been trying to persuade my fellow directors to embrace a convergence between linear and interactive storytelling and technologies. Bryan has a hope: 'We need a Mexican film director to come back home and use the tech!' (Bryan Steagall). Let's hope this happens. Indeed, there is one green shoot in that direction, director Guillermo del Toro has set up an animation school in Guadalajara – the Centro Internacional de Animación.

Meanwhile, in New Zealand, a more positive view is offered:

Actors need to expand their capabilities and not just look for films and shorts. They need to do their homework and research – approaching studios and interactive companies and finding out who has been greenlit. Most animators don't understand actors and that they need them, so actors should approach animators as they need physical performers. We need actors to seek out the emerging tech and ask to work. The currency of trust is more important than money. Actors need to get a portfolio. It's important to get used to the word 'no' – it should be used as an opportunity. It may be that the people you approach do not understand what is possible.

JEASY SEGHAL

In the classes Pascal and I have run, we have always encouraged our students to be self-motivated and to approach studios and universities with mocap studios to offer their services. Though in the UK this may no longer be such a successful route due to increased competition, it certainly makes sense in both New Zealand and Latin America. I suspect that it will apply to other countries with a developing mocap industry. Go out and find your collaborators and persuade games and VR developers, animation studios and mocap tech firms what you can do and how much value an actor can bring. We have examples from many countries of actors doing just that and getting valuable experience and potentially showreel material in the process.

Before you get into a downer about the state of the industry in your part of the world, here are some words of positivity from someone doing it for years: 'In my experience as a teacher some actors say they only want to do mocap! Though it's hard to get into and you have to prove yourself, it is clear there is a real lure – a chance to really use your imagination' (Richard Dorton).

How equal are the opportunities?

We believe the mocap stage is the ideal place for a true meritocracy. You are there, first and foremost, because you are useful. Ideally – a 'multi-tool'. It's a question of access in the social context of the outside world. That's why we advocate training, spreading information and knowledge to ensure a true meritocracy as well as getting rid of closed-shop and over-powerful unions who can have their own filtering effect. Anyway, that's an ideal – but what of the reality on the ground?

> In mocap it's never mattered what you look like. For example, it's taken a long time for TV and commercials to cast men with beards and interracial relationships. When Black Lives Matter started in 2020, as a mixed-race person, I thought about the fact I've broken that barrier from the beginning. I never felt like there was any pressure on me – I broke the ethnic mould early on and helped to create conditions that are now more open minded. If you make a conscious choice to promote diversity it reflects well on that company. We should be making more effort to use Black actors to play Black characters and we have to address this in society – it's not a political correctness thing, it's the right thing to do.
>
> RICHARD DORTON

One of the game developers I'm working with at the moment is working on inclusion and diversity in the game and we are having active discussions about representation and needing to cast faithfully to racial type. 'These days developers are often not looking for cut and paste actors, so we can look for more diversity' (Jessica Jefferies). Though it's true that it doesn't matter what you look like in mocap because the data doesn't detect racial background, it has taken something as seismic as the Black Lives Matter movement to force the issue and make developers and broadcasters responsible for what they put on screen regarding diversity and how they cast for those roles.

Richard Dorton has been part of a gathering debate that has made race and representation matter in mocap casting. We have cautious hope for a future in which a technology that sees past skin colour can influence the decision makers who use it. We would like to think that this book will play its part in encouraging those currently either unrepresented or under-represented to make a go of it and inspire a wider range of people to become involved, irrespective of social position, class, geographical location and race.

What are the games developers, casting directors and directors looking for?

When I'm casting for In-game, I'm looking for skill – skilled movement and talented people with stunt ability etc. For cinematics I'm looking for the best actor, putting together a cast that will work well together. Sometimes it's just a feeling, an opportunity presents itself, I felt they deserved that break and they proved themselves. Some haven't and have not been asked back. If you have someone with skills but who is a terrible person, you have to balance it with what will work. Some people work with the same people all the time. To me, every job is situational – a gut feeling.

RICHARD DORTON

As we've mentioned before, the collaborative nature of mocap, combined with the frenetic pace of most schedules, means there is little room for big egos or the individual over the group. Eventually, being uncollaborative can catch up with even the biggest film and TV stars, but in mocap it happens faster. You won't get asked back if you don't fit into the team.

As well as being a collaborator, flexibility is also a requirement:

You have to be open but also be ready to change things. In VR, I ask them to perform directly to the camera because that's what the player will get – it can be a very alien experience for actors. You need to be able to go with the flow. I worked on a big game for DC, all hidden by NDAs. I had to write scenes and character descriptions that were similar to the characters but set in a different world. Actors came in with a clear idea of these constructed characters. If I needed to see something different then it threw some of them and exposed their inflexibility. You need to be flexible. Due to NDAs you need to be willing to be flexible and be as open as possible. There is no cut and paste way of getting in. It should be treated with the same respect as traditional media.

JESSICA JEFFERIES

So, you need to be collaborative and flexible. What else?

I look for – not mandatory but it helps – people who have a sense of rhythm and pacing in the way they walk and talk, people who can register three or four different technical and performance notes and act on that. People who have a background in dancing or martial arts, as they have a sense of rhythm and pose. More often, because we are in sci-fi or horror, you need people who look good carrying a weapon on or can hit a hero pose. People who have done a creature workshop, that is always helpful.

STEVE KNIEBIHLY

Here you will remember what I said in the previous chapter about being able to take different notes – technical, blocking and character. As a director, I have often looked into an actor's eyes and fervently hoped I haven't bamboozled them completely with my notes and that their glazed expression is not an indication of total confusion! In a mocap studio there may be many voices, so going back to your core acting ethos, being centred and able to filter out what you do and don't need, knowing what you require to hit specifications and expectations, and then surpass them, is key.

Following the notion that taking technical and character notes is important, here's a thought to push that further: '[What's important is] body control – being able to do the same motion over and over again. If you act with a different emotion, it can change the feel of the take. You have to imagine the costume and weapons and the environment' (Yuji Shimomura). When I talked to Yuji, there was a distinct feel of someone working in two cultures – coming from Japan and then sometimes working often with Western talent. What was the difference? What was he looking for?

> The instincts are different and the rhythm they have in their bodies. *Meri & Hari* – the Japanese term which is hard to explain – but it's about quick and slow, stillness and movement. In Japanese heroic movies there is a prelude, a stillness and then they hit the pose. We have a certain rhythm. It starts with Kabuki (*Mie**) and period drama. Western actors have a different rhythm. It can be hard to make them do it the same as a Japanese actor. The important thing is to collaborate with them to make something new. I want to use Western actors because they have something Japanese don't have and the challenge comes if they need to incorporate more of the *Meri & Hari* approach. In action and drama we used the motion more to emphasise the stillness and vice versa.
>
> YUJI SHIMOMURA

The **Mie* is a pose that sums the character up, which happens at an emotional and dramatic peak. You might call it a kind of 'base pose'.

Meri & Hari is a Japanese concept that teaches us to keep the correct balance between tension and relaxation. In Japan there is a tradition that we must not carry today's troubles and tiredness till tomorrow. At the end of each day, we should find time to relax. We should not study or work until we fall asleep. We should have some relaxed time at the end of the day. '*Merihari no aru*' is the opposite of 'monotonous' and 'boring'. If you were playing a tune on your piano, the tone should not be dull, but you should play it with a lot of gusto where needed, and quiet and elegantly where that is needed, so giving it a good contrast.

All the experts I interviewed have specific things they are looking for. Do your research, understand what medium, cultural expectations and genre they are looking for before you go in. Having said that, the most common word that represents what they are all looking for seems to be – collaboration.

A note on whether you need to train – or not!

Given that we are people who believe in teaching people the basics of mocap so they understand what to expect in the volume, what follows next is something perhaps both surprising and perhaps controversial, but I'm going to add it because I believe in trying to represent an array of views from a diverse variety of voices. I also know the speaker as a serious, talented and busy director of mocap and performance capture. I asked Kate Saxon about the skills required: 'Thinking about performers in mocap, what are you looking for in a mocap actor? What specific skills and experience do they need to have?' She answered with this:

> I feel really strongly about this: none – no specific skills and experience. I think there's a myth that's built up in the industry that has scared a lot of actors away from video games: namely believing that they

require specialist training first. In my opinion, this is frankly nonsense. Many actors have spent an arm and a leg putting themselves through drama school – so they are trained as an actor already, as are those who've learnt their trade on the job. Mocap requires nothing other than good acting. A good actor is a good actor in whatever medium: whether it be TV, theatre, film, radio, or video games. I've been directing games now for about seventeen years and I've cast actors who've never done mocap before, more often than I've cast actors who have. It's very easy to learn the tricks of the trade on the job and I find it takes literally only minutes of rehearsal before an actor is relaxed in the environment. One of my jobs is to guide the cast through the specific technical requirements of a mocap volume, and I'm always happy to advise on any aspects that require explanation. Crews at mocap stages are also excellent at demystifying the tech. So, in regards to what I look for in performers of mocap, it's the same that I look for when casting any role in any medium (I direct games, TV and theatre), and that's suitability for the character, talent and an eagerness to take risks. Which basically equates to eagerness to make strong choices and invest in a role, and be prepared to step over the line of 'safety' to push themselves to achieve more in that role. Of course, if an actor feels they'd like to experience a mocap volume prior to a job, and therefore sign up for a course, then I imagine it will be useful for them, but it is not a necessity.

KATE SAXON

As this book has shown, we have a different view, but Kate knows her stuff and has a lot of experience. We have seen the students at the classes we have taught grow in understanding and confidence in how to succeed in the mocap studio – many of whom won't get the chance to work with a director as actor focused and supportive as Kate. We've also heard stories of those who get little or no direction, in which case their training has been there to support them. We believe in the notion that actors who want to sustain a career should understand the technical demands of their chosen medium, just as Michael Caine will talk about understanding lenses and field of view in film so as to moderate the size of his performance and blocking, and voice specialists will teach vocal projection so those in the cheap seats at big theatres can hear the actor. We also fervently believe that digital performance mediums – mocap, VR and animation – need a focused corporeal understanding, a link between psychology and movement that remains absent for many actors, even those graduating from drama schools.

A good actor in one medium may be uncomfortable and not have the skills for another medium. Not every actor can sing, or excel at voice work. As Gilles Monteil notes, not every actor has enough physical awareness to tell a story nonverbally as themselves, let alone a character in a high stakes situation. But that same actor might be great in a medical drama series. But what Kate says is echoed by Richard Dorton – what he is looking for is a good actor and that is the most important thing. Once you have a good actor, they can learn the specific technical requirements.

Just to compound this notion and lay out the basic expectations, here is a very clear summation from a mocap casting director:

Here are the three main things I believe actors need to remember –

1   Connection. You must be connected to the ground and physically connected for a full body performance.
2   Breath. Unlike the screen, you can't tell the story with your eyes, you need to use breath. Breath will tell us whenever you are excited or nervous etc. The underlying breath in the Avatar always gives it life.
3   Imagination. You may well be in an enormous room, wearing Lycra® with a bucket. Your imagination has to do the rest. For

three years of my life I worked on 'Until Dawn' and I spent most of that walking around with a bucket as a lantern!

JESSICA JEFFERIES

How to decide what skills and training you should consider

If you decide that you do need to look for training, what follows are some suggestions.

Our recommendations should be considered for skills that you believe will benefit you personally and professionally *in all* media according to the context and local industry you are in. These guidelines focus on aspects that help develop the skills we identify in this book as important for mocap work, not in any way excluding the vital role regular acting training plays.

If the industry you have access to has a need for particular skills, it may be useful to train in those areas. Martial arts, stage combat, military manoeuvres, and gun handling fall into these categories. Please remember that *solely* focusing on these skills can compromise your physical freedom required by embodied acting, as Pascal Langdale points out at the beginning of this book.

Training in techniques that allow for freedom of movement and improvisation will ensure you don't train your body to only follow particular shapes and movements. Schools and systems to consider will ally themselves with the teachers and schools mentioned in Chapter 2 or will have these same priorities: The improvement of proprioception and kinesthesia, improvisation and nonverbal storytelling.

As mentioned above, drama and acting schools are responding slowly to the needs of digital performance, as are film schools – they are sometimes decades behind where the industry is. Having said that, we have found that actors who have been drama school-trained tend to find working in mocap a relatively natural progression, so if you are able to find an acting course that encompasses and is open to animation and acting corporeally, then it is worth considering. Remember, as Richard Dorton says, acting for mocap is *acting – be a good actor* first and foremost.

Getting granular – how do I submit for a job?

Let's talk about casting first. You might get into the room, you might not. Of course, there are distinct advantages to self-taping – it now doesn't matter so much where you are based and it has been of particular use in this time of the Covid pandemic. Having a clear and decent space, well lit, without background distractions, making sure your body and outline stands out clearly will help.

A wide shot allows me to see physicality and I expect you to be uninhibited with your performance. You need to go back to your training and explore and use your craft. I want to see your imagination and I need to see and believe you are in a desert even if it's a freezing cold Studio with a bucket! For performance capture, a head and shoulders shot is useful to hone in on voice and face and make sure you have enough facial movement to drive the facial rig. A full body shot is still important and it often throws people. I need to see a full body shot in order to see you are 100 per cent present. It can really expose people or conversely some find it very freeing with no props or set to get in the way.

JESSICA JEFFERIES

Figure 9.1 *'For performance capture, a head and shoulders shot is useful to hone in on voice and face and make sure you have enough facial movement to drive the facial rig' (Jessica Jefferies). (Photo by Archis Achrekar.)*

Jessica is a relative rarity in that, as a casting director, she specializes in mocap. The situation is a little different in LA, though you'll find some of the same requirements. Richard Dorton explains:

> Some say you should shoot 'cowboy', which is also known as a medium long shot, knee to head. I like to see it full body. If it's P-cap, a medium shot can be useful. It depends on the scene you are given. If they're not being scanned, I need to see more. It's really hard to believe a digital close-up performance so we need to see the whole body ... I like wider shots – why would you cut off the feet? Often it comes from a traditional casting approach. Casting is sometimes done by trusted casting directors many of whom do TV, film and games. There are a few who have done a lot of games too and they know what is needed. I cast for a lot of games but also

other media. I would never cast a stunt heavy job with a singer! There are no pure mocap casting directors I know of in LA. I know of one manager who has a mocap list. Some voice agents have a mocap division. I don't believe there should be dedicated agents, managers or casting directors who do only mocap. We need more mocap casting knowledge. But we need to be casting good actors first and foremost. I can't compete with the top casting directors, but I have had the experience of going up for a creature part and was shot at the casting with a close-up of my face! Many casting directors still don't get mocap!

RICHARD DORTON

One thing that is really important is to get into the heads of the casting director and the director. How long is your attention span? How quickly do you decide whether you want to keep watching a film, TV show or YouTube video? Not long, right? Casting requires going

Figure 9.2 *'It's really hard to believe a digital close-up performance so we need to see the whole body' (Richard Dorton). (Photo by Archis Achrekar.)*

through multiple, sometimes hundreds, of clips. How quickly are most rejection decisions made? In a matter of seconds – just like you when you change channels. And in case you think in person castings are much different, quite often the decision has been made as you walk through the door or not long after. So, make sure your scenes start well, you make clear and bold decisions and you make that entrance that represents the character you want to show. Put yourself in the position of the viewer. Is your effort worthy of serious consideration? Is it worth watching the whole scene? Casting directors and directors are looking for reasons to say no – can you imagine how hard it is for them to decide between a large number of candidates for a role? The bar is high, expectations and standards are high, and you have to cut the mustard from the get go. It's true that you just might not fit the image of what they are looking for, but the important thing is to give your best shot with what you have. You can do no more.

And speaking of doing no more, don't do more than required. It's quality, not quantity. Whenever I look at a casting clip and it runs to several minutes I inwardly sigh. I think 'this better be good . . .!' This applies to showreels too. Actors are supposed to be good at understanding and empathizing. Think about who is watching. These days my directing showreels are shorter than ever before for a good reason – attention spans are shorter and precious time is rarer. You don't have to have one showreel. Have one for movement, one that highlights your special skills – combat, dance, parkour, weapons etc. Have a separate one for drama scenes. Follow the tips above, make them short and dynamic – once your reel starts, make it compelling so the viewer has to keep watching. Don't repeat yourself – make your editing snappy. I watch far too many showreels that I feel outstay their welcome and are indulgent. Show yours to your friends and get some opinions. Get them put together by someone who knows how to edit.

Invest in your reels – they are your calling card, your statement of intent! If you are sending it to an animator, they are probably going to want to see the way you move, the way you walk – make sure your material shows that. If it's for cinematics, make sure your reel shows off your acting chops.

If you have material of yourself in a mocap suit, in the volume or wearing an inertial suit, so much the better. Then it's clear that you have experience. If not, don't despair. But with all that you have learnt from this book, make sure you are showing off your physical acting and environmental skills clearly. A reel full of broody film close ups might look super sexy to you and your friends, but it's not much use to show off your mocap potential!

Chapter 9 takeaways

Mocap is proving its worth	Motion capture performance is beginning to be taken seriously by industries other than just games.
How has the industry changed in your part of the world?	Motion capture has come a long way and the opportunities, particularly for women, are opening up. In New Zealand and Latin America, green shoots are growing also. From Japanese VTubers, to VR, AR and the stage, the use of mocap is expanding worldwide. Meanwhile, government support and education is playing catch up.
So how do we find work?	Though the picture varies, there are opportunities for those who have determination and an entrepreneurial spirit.
How equal are the opportunities?	Mocap has the potential to be a true meritocracy and diversity is starting to be encouraged.

What are the games developers, casting directors and directors looking for?	Understanding the creative requirements, genre and culture is essential, but all seem to agree on the value of collaboration and lack of ego.
A note on whether you need to train – or not!	For some, training may not be needed, but for others it is valuable. A corporeal understanding is essential as is to be a good actor.
How to decide what skills and training you should consider	Though specific skills might be required for certain jobs, an overall training that teaches the qualities we discuss in Chapter 3 is important in supporting embodiment and corporeal skills.
Getting granular – how do I submit for a job?	Use your powers of empathy to understand the mind of the casting director. Make your showreel and casting tapes short and to the point. Framing is important so make sure you understand what the casting director expects.

Notes

1   Clayton Davis, 'Top 10 Best Motion Capture Performances in Film'. *Variety*, 20 April 2021. https://variety.com/lists/best-motion-capture-characters-andy-serkis/

2   Ibid.

10

What will the landscape be in ten years' time? A low wager bet between professional futurists . . .

PASCAL LANGDALE

Motion capture has developed massively since it began to be used in animation in video games less than forty years ago. Over the time the contributors to this book have worked in the medium, the landscape has changed in terms of technology, ambition, diversity and the sheer breadth of uses the technology is facilitating. Where will this technology be taking us in the coming decade and what is the actor's place in the new world? Actors will need to stay abreast of current trends and tech in the medium across platforms old and new. Which brings us right back to why we wanted to write this book in the first place.

Contributors – Alex Coulombe (co-founder of Agile Lens), Kim Baumann Larsen (XR producer and virtual reality architect/CEO and founder of Dimension Design), Ben Lumsden (business development manager, Epic Games), Jeremy Meunier (motion capture lead at MOOV, Squeeze Animation) and Stéphane Dalbera (founder and owner of Atopos).

The state of play

At time of writing there is much excitement over Epic's release of *MetaHumans*, making available high-fidelity facial animation free for use with Unreal Engine. As revolutionary as this may be, it will be surpassed soon enough. In this chapter we take a look at the general direction of the technology, the increasing use in media other than game and film, and the resulting changing role of the actor in an expanding industry.

Figure 10.1 *'Epic Games' MetaHuman Creator was made available for free in 2021. (© Epic Games.)*

Ben Lumsden, business development manager for Unreal use in anything beyond games, is naturally excited about the 'metaverse', which he describes as 'a cross between the Matrix and Ready Player One'. The idea is that interactive entertainment will be developed and collectively played or experienced by a global audience entirely in the cloud. Elements of *Amazon* and *Fortnite* are examples of the developing metaverse.

> In the next ten to twenty years we'll see another revolution: varied forms of entertainment with interactivity and agency involved with an open source ecosystem like the internet. Had the internet been made by one organisation then it would be s****. Tim [Sweeney, Epic's founder and CEO] is about making the engine free to use and the metaverse becoming completely available to everyone.
>
> BEN LUMSDEN

Epic is backing motion capture as a key part of the metaverse toolset. Whether you are working on a virtual set with an LED screen, outside in the elements, or providing a room-based VR experience, if you are being placed in a virtual world you will need to track motion.

When we ask about future advances in motion capture, there doesn't seem to be much anticipation of great change, except in democratization. Volumetric capture will move into real time eventually but will remain accessible only to the deepest pockets for some time. This will be the capture of choice, when a high-fidelity 3D reproduction of the actor's face is desired. Imagine famous actors having their seminal performance of a famous theatre play recorded for all time in volumetric detail. Audience members could get closer to the action than the front seats and, in some cases, there might be a market for living actors to perform with the legacy performer long after the original star has died. In contrast, inertial systems are now accessible to passionate amateurs, indie developers and tech savvy actors. They have their challenges, but the opportunities for grass roots development and service provision has grown exponentially in the past two years alone at the time of writing and looks set to continue.

There will be noticeable changes due to advancements in artificial intelligence or AI. The number of markers required to define a skeleton will go down, reducing both the price point and the sheer hassle of marker placement. Procedural animation will increasingly be used to animate non-player character interactions and generic behaviours, not just locomotions. The theme seems to be that software in the foreseeable future will primarily improve the quality and the user experience of existing processes.

These advances will mean changes to the actor's landscape, closing some doors and opening others. The rules of how to find work in motion capture, established over the past decade, are changing and with change comes opportunity.

Expanding use of motion capture

In 2011 I worked with a small mocap company to present a real-time animated excerpt from Shakespeare's *The Tempest*, for Canada 3.0, in Stratford Ontario (home of Canada's Shakespeare Festival Theatre). The optical system crashed more than once, the graphics were basic, and I was wearing an early version of the Dynamixyz single view HMC using visible light. In 2014 I co-wrote and co-produced a live interactive theatre drama, *Faster Than Night*, projecting an animation driven by facial capture on a large screen beside me. That required a tech team of two and had basic graphics and, although occasionally buggy, the system didn't crash. In 2018 the Royal Shakespeare

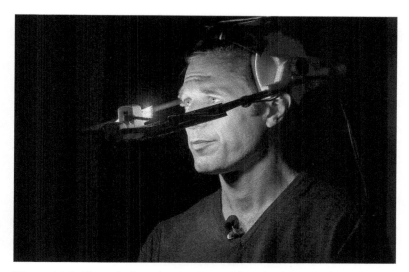

Figure 10.2 *Theatrical production* Faster Than Night. *Pascal Langdale in 2014 wearing a Dynamixyz SV HMC. (Dynamixyz – A Take-Two division. Photo by John Jacques.)*

Company used motion capture in a full-length production of *The Tempest*, motion capturing the character Ariel. In 2021, an R&D production by the same company produced a live animated, slightly interactive play called *Dream* to host mocapped magical spirits played by half a dozen actors. Unreal's real-time engine was now inserting the characters and a virtual world inspired by *A Midsummer Night's Dream*, with real-time weather effects and rustling leaves, and ray tracing (which helps create directional light) the systems now robust enough to be relied on.

In a single decade, the quality and accessibility of the technology have improved to the point that theatres are increasingly looking to mocap to help tell stories. But things are going even further. There is now increasing use of that other revolutionary upstart, VR.

If you go back to 2016, which was the launch of the first commercial headsets, we have come a long way .... New headsets are available in the Facebook labs with very realistic VR. But you need machine learning to add nuances you don't get from current tech. In five to ten years we will have headsets which will allow facial performances, so you can look like yourself – though, why would you want to?

KIM BAUMANN LARSEN

The VR headset is beginning to offer player expressive facial tracking with the Vive facial tracker, particularly powerful when using a headset with eye tracking like the Vive Pro Eye. If facial capture whilst wearing a VR headset is not yet universally available, the body is well on its way. As far back as 2017, Alex Coulombe was developing custom VR experiences that tracked hands through the controllers, and feet with Vive trackers. Alex was rewarded with a surprising level of expressivity from actors willing to explore how to confer emotion only with head position, hands and feet. There are now inertial suits and software that, from these points alone, can even interpolate a close match to body position.

Challenges in the new world

Kim Baumann Larsen asks, why would a normal consumer want to see their own face in a virtual world? Perhaps it is to do with presence, seeing you have presence in the virtual fiction you are being asked to experience or play in. In contrast, wearing a digital 'mask' is key to the success of the VTubers mentioned in Chapter 9. This is a sticky problem – one that so far hasn't had a solution other than allowing the customization of your avatar's outfit. Lucrative, but not enough. If a million people are playing or engaging in your world, they want to see the effect of their interaction, they want to know they exist, that their presence counts. This is why game designers are rightfully obsessed with serving the player, and giving them every chance to affect the world, or even the course of the narrative, of the game. And once a player can interact and be seen (as themselves *or* an avatar) in a shared virtual world, where does this leave the actor? Doesn't the audience become the hero of their own story, and everyone else a supporting cast member?

Good facial tracking and animation whilst wearing a VR headset will not be available on a consumer level for some time, so actors may be employed to act on their behalf. The developer might record reactions, or emotions, that can be applied to faces of the audience in their virtual role as supporting cast member. This would support and augment emotionally consistent interactions between participants' avatars in the virtual scene. Specially created libraries of actor gestures and expressions may be built to provide the basis for these procedurally animated characters – acting *on behalf* of the audience member, for the benefit of all the other participants around them. As in game development, once the library is created the actor is in less demand for that kind of contribution, at least on that production.

At the other end of the scale, digital doublage and deep fakes allow for another encroachment on the current range of work available to actors. In previous years, no famous actor would accept a job in a game, not even a cinematic. As both the graphic fidelity and the narrative quality have improved, stars are finding their brand has value and credibility in the new medium. If non-player characters are increasingly procedurally animated, and stars and established high-profile figures are taking the cinematic roles, where does the jobbing actor fit in? And that's not even considering the re-animation of deceased actors! But don't despair. As with previous industrial and technological revolutions, new opportunities appear where old practices decline.

Opportunities in a new world

Recently, a film director I worked with, Randall Okita, wrote, directed and appeared in a cross media VR documentary. Part personal journey, part interactive puzzle game, Randall is a good example of a creative mindset ready for the next era in storytelling. He is one of a new wave of cross-discipline creatives around the globe who are testing, failing and succeeding, in their attempts to understand how to tell stories and play games, in a 3D, interactive, virtual immersive experience. The potential of virtual platforms to tell stories is becoming increasingly accepted by a new generation, who have grown up in a world playing games. What now some may see as a logical option, a decade ago was considered niche at best, low aspiration at worst. Now, there are VR theatre experiences designed for one audience member; others that employ actors in VR headset sets in different time zones to improvise with audience members. The sheer range of skills and art forms required in this field is astounding – theatre, film, storytelling, game, animation, art, music, design and programming are just the more obvious.

One aspect of live interactive VR seems consistent. Alex Coulombe (co-founder, Agile Lens) is an advocate of improvisation and has hired comedians in dramatic roles because of their ability to improvise with members of the public, and still deliver narrative goals, or 'yes and …' responses to technical glitches. Perhaps tellingly and in keeping with the theme of this book, this was an ability he had found lacking in classically trained actors.

Historically, though, there have been other attempts at what can therefore be fairly described as total art (*Gesamtkunstwerk*, a term coined by classical composer Wilhelm Wagner (b. 1813), meaning literally 'total work of art'). However, the current level of access to the tools and necessary training is unparalleled in the human experience. Wagner would have a ball today.

The Germans may need to invent a new word for 'total *global* work of art' to describe a new level of audience/participant reach. 'Pixel streaming' means only the image is held on the client device. All the processing is done remotely. All contributors to a production, including actors, can work from anywhere in the world collaborating in the same virtual space.

Entertainment has always used technology to create illusions, whether that be wind effects in a Victorian Shakespeare production, or a high-fidelity CGI hormone-button-pressing-tent-pole-blockbuster-summer-movie. Once entertainment fully moves into the metaverse, entertainment experiences can then be individualized on a massive scale. Therefore, the currency of entertainment will be the sense of connection to other humans/players, not a connection with an AI, which will quickly lose its novelty. Animation and special effects may mediate this human connection, but it will not be its own justification. Any story or game must always justify the choice of platform it uses, not the other way around – or you're just a solution looking for a problem. The best experiences will continue to be justified by speaking to our shared fear, bravery or hope. We are most engaged when we see these aspects of ourselves, aspects of our lives, however basic, in the entertainment we consume.

In the mocap volume the actor is the human element delivering a small chaos and unpredictability. Jeremy Meunier and Stéphane Dalbera note that this chaos can be misperceived as 'noise' – movements that are perceived as undesired as they don't seem smooth or consistent with the desired move. This can be microscopic or large scale. Jeremy continues that the trick to mocap data clean-up is to make sure you leave the noise of the human in, otherwise the result is stripped of what makes the performance relatable. This being so, it follows that the actor must rise to the challenge and always be more interesting than any AI driven alternative. Moreover, the actor's ability to improvise and, improvise *live*, promises to be the distinguishing factor and has the potential of great currency.

The next decade will test these theories out, but one thing remains true. As we stated at the outset of this book, if you are not involved and current with the evolution and demands of your craft in this area, you stand to be left behind.

Everyone we have talked to has suggested that the future of the metaverse, the future of the games we play, the stories we tell and the blend of the two, are dependent on an industry now finally poised to launch from the grass roots level. The consistent prediction is that, instead of accessing work in a mocap volume through a standard casting for a big video game or film company, work will increasingly be found with, and created by, small teams of independent creatives and animators. The advice is to find start-ups or students working on their showcases and offer the creative skills you have as a collaborator. It's worth repeating a quote from Jeasy here:

> The currency of trust is more important than money. Actors need to get a portfolio.
>
> JEASY SEGHAL

If you have an idea, but lack the technical or animation skills, then team up with someone who does. Don't wait for the old industry to find you. Become the next generation challenging the assumptions and business models of today, using the same tools, but free from the binding legacy of what's worked so far. Mocap in entertainment has always been about going beyond what is possible. Now go even further. Manifest the impossible.

Chapter 10 takeaways

Mocap is expanding into a new age	The skills you will need have to meet the demands of motion capture in an increasing range of storytelling and game platforms.
The future will reward grass roots creators	Make connections, build trust and a portfolio with small teams, universities, students, and independents. Don't rely on getting 'that big job' with a major game company or film.

Appendix: Chapter by Chapter Summary

Chapter 1: What is motion capture?

History of performance styles	Humans have been performing corporeally for centuries. Religion limited it. Silent movies brought it back. Animation and mocap require performers to use the skills of old in this most contemporary medium.
Digital and virtual production	Mocap has been born out of the reality of digital and virtual production, facilitated by the development of real-time engines and video games. Interactive storytelling has now become mainstream.
Mocap – the technical lowdown	Whether optical, line-of-sight, inertial or markerless mocap, all capture the skeleton, but performance capture also captures the voice and face.
The performer as puppeteer	A first taste of the challenges ahead of using the performer's body to drive the digital skeleton, which in turn puppets the skin of the animated avatar character.

Chapter 2: The body

Train	Hone your muscle memory, and senses of proprioception and kinesthesia, for effortless and complete physical control.
Learn about you	Transcend your own physical heritage so it doesn't show up in your character.
Nonverbal storytelling	Through real-life observation and practice, learn how to tell the dramatic story you want to the audience/player.
Commit	Put your efforts into truthfully embodying the character or creature – physically, emotionally and psychologically.

Chapter 3: Imaginary environments

Train your imagination	It's a muscle. It improves and strengthens with practice. Read *To the Actor: On the Technique of Acting* by Michael Chekhov.
Use your senses	Don't imagine every leaf on every tree, use your senses to evoke and pull you into the imaginary environment.
Find the drama	Develop your sense of drama in nonverbal storytelling: mask work is recommended.
Corporeal mime	Every second is a chance to physically tell the story so make the invisible world physically visible with clear intentions. For example, if you turn your head to look at something, know what demanded your attention.

Chapter 4: Mocap is an animated medium

What is our job in an animated medium?	We have to understand the needs of the animator to create characters that appear to be bestowed with life.

The mocap pipeline	We outline the process as: acquisition, cleaning, solving, retargeting and finally finished animation.
Capturing facial performance	Facial capture is probably the most complex and expensive part of the technology and requires truthful and dynamic performances.
The eye of the animator	Despite the technological complexity of the pipeline, there is a surprising amount of interpretation and artistry involved in creating great animation from mocap.
The animators' relationship with the actor	Many animators are not used to working with actors. Understanding the process, and your role, will help you understand and collaborate with the animator.
The difference between motion capture and performance capture in animation	Animators use different processes and combinations of capture to create performances, from combining multiple parts of a performance to capturing a single actor's total performance in one go in performance capture. In contrast, mocap generally means no facial capture.
Digital makeup versus augmented animation	Animators point at the reality of the mocap pipeline, as involving much more creative input than just 'makeup'.
What animators are looking for in an actor	The technical and physical characteristics necessary for doing the job from the animator's perspective, the relationship between voice and body capture, and how physical traits affect performance whether lead roles or NPCs.
The shoot	More cameras than crew, more variation in who is directing you, see-through furniture, sets and proxy stand-in props and drawn out and sporadic schedules.

Chapter 5: Building a character in motion capture

Embody	Don't get restricted to either 'outside-in' or 'inside-out'. Use whatever techniques that work to have a physically, emotionally and psychologically integrated character. If it works, it works.

Explore	Learn and practise Laban, Lecoq's pull/push, silhouettes, animal studies, approach/avoid.
Quick access tools	Never forget it in your checklist and use these as a key to hit the ground running: breath, rhythm and music.
Always act	Even if you know your capture data is unlikely to be useful (creature work for example), still deliver your best performance possible from initial to end 'T-pose'. You are a primary team member who shares creative responsibility with the animator. Ask questions to get the answers you need.

Chapter 6: Video game locomotion

The player is controller and audience	'Locomotions' – all the routine movements from walking to gun handling – need to be captured and animated. This normally makes up the majority of any game experience.
Locomotions are technical	You need great physical awareness and control to match positions and create symmetrical movements, working within character restraints and shapes.
Locomotions need some character	The animation director will help decide how much character. However, your character choices need to be applicable in as wide a range of circumstances as possible and always filled with the energy of goal-oriented intention.
It's a workout of repetition	You can perform hundreds of moves in a day, some can require remarkable endurance. Change the order of shot list to deliver the best results. Negotiate with other actors for the best compromise.

Chapter 7: Cinematics

Directing cinematics is different from other media	The performance director's position and status in the process varies in different projects.

What are cinematics?	Cinematics are dramatic scenes and the stakes are always high, interactivity is key and the relationship with the player crucial.
How are cinematics created?	Whether prescriptive in terms of fulfilling previs, or more freeing, the performer needs to deliver what the animator and director need.
A note on preparation	Whether you have rehearsal time or no time at all to prepare, or NDAs hamper information flow, flexibility is key.
Mocap, facial capture, performance capture and working with pre-recorded audio	With an understanding of the many different permutations of capture and why and when they occur – which can create the 'Frankenstein effect' – you will have a better idea of how to modulate your performance. Acting to someone else's voice can be surprisingly inspiring.
How does interaction in a scene affect performance?	Understanding the player's interaction in a scene and the needs of the game developers to support gameplay will help you deliver in the volume.
Cameras in cinematics	There are different cameras that you will encounter in the volume – infra-red, reference/witness and virtual cameras. The virtual camera can free things up and can separate the performance from the camera.
The vibe in a mocap studio	It is very different to work in a mocap studio compared with film and stage. There tends to be more gender equality, and collaborative and ego-free behaviour is both valued and expected.

Chapter 8: Direction and the lack of it

Expectations of the director	The director's job is to be the representative of the viewer/payer or audience. If they are not present, this becomes your responsibility.

The different types of mocap work	There are many different types of director you will encounter in mocap. You'll likely be working on several projects over a long time. Self-reliance, 100 per cent commitment, good organization and practice are essential.
What kind of information do you get before arriving at the studio?	While the amount of information you get prior to a mocap shoot varies, your preparedness and knowing what information you yourself need to work quickly will help to deal with the challenge.
How often are you directed by a director?	By developing a strong outside eye and understanding the perspective of the viewer, you will increase independence and deliver better performances.
More on working with pre-recorded voice.	Actors can use pre-recorded voice as inspiration, including an exercise where you can try to recreate a performance of an actor you admire.
How has mocap changed?	The status of performers in mocap has changed significantly for the better. Maintaining a positive attitude will help you become more employable.

Chapter 9: The industry – finding your place in a new medium

Mocap is proving its worth	Motion capture performance is beginning to be taken seriously by industries other than just games.
How has the industry changed in your part of the world?	Motion capture has come a long way and the opportunities, particularly for women, are opening up. In New Zealand and Latin America, green shoots are growing also. From Japanese VTubers to VR, AR and the stage, the use of mocap is expanding worldwide. Meanwhile, Government support and education is playing catch up.
So how do we find work?	Though the picture varies, there are opportunities for those who have determination and an entrepreneurial spirit.

How equal are the opportunities?	Mocap has the potential to be a true meritocracy and diversity is starting to be encouraged.
What are the games developers, casting directors and directors looking for?	Understanding the creative requirements, genre and culture is essential, but all seem to agree on the value of collaboration and lack of ego.
A note on whether you need to train – or not!	For some, training may not be needed, but for others it is valuable. A corporeal understanding is essential as is to be a good actor.
How to decide what skills and training you should consider	Though specific skills might be required for certain jobs, an overall training that teaches the qualities we discuss in Chapter 3 is important in supporting embodiment and corporeal skills.
Getting granular – how do I submit for a job?	Use your powers of empathy to understand the mind of the casting director. Make your showreel and casting tapes short and to the point. Framing is important so make sure you understand what the casting director expects.

Chapter 10: What will the landscape be in ten years' time?

Mocap is expanding into a new age	The skills you will need have to meet the demands of motion capture in an increasing range of storytelling and game platforms.
The future will reward grass roots creators	Make connections, build trust and a portfolio with small teams, universities, students and independents. Don't rely on getting 'that big job' with a major game company or film.

Index

www.ingramcontent.com/pod-product-compliance
Ingram Content Group UK Ltd.
Pitfield, Milton Keynes, MK11 3LW, UK
UKHW020733280225

455688UK00012B/628